'Matthew's Gospel is a major reaso.
Church opted to keep all four Gospels rather than merge them into one "life of Jesus", which would have hidden the fact that real life and faith can arouse deep and passionate arguments and differences. We each have our own way of seeing. Nevertheless, from those differences we are led to deeper levels of understanding about ourselves and the meaning of faith.

I am very grateful that in *Meeting God in Matthew*, Elaine Storkey brings us back to thinking through many of those issues afresh, as well as opening up the text of Matthew's Gospel in such a clear and relevant way.'
Ronald Clements, Professor Emeritus of Old Testament Studies, King's College London

'With her light touch and self-effacing style, Elaine Storkey leads us gently and winsomely through Matthew's Gospel to meet with Jesus. Matthew, evangelist and student, recognized Jesus' central role in Jewish and human history. His Gospel begins and ends with the assurance that God is with us. Always.

Reaching across the centuries, treading lightly on scholarship, Elaine the teacher invites us to meet Jesus the Teacher, as interpreted by Matthew the teacher. The Jesus we meet is the one through whom God is always with us. This book is down-to-earth, accessible, illuminating. I loved it.'
The Right Reverend Jill Duff, Bishop of Lancaster

'The field of biblical studies has flooded the market with multiple commentaries. When another appears, I instinctively react with, "Oh no, not another one!". Let me assure you that this book does not fall into that category.

Elaine Storkey approaches Matthew step by step in a topical manner, and yet, remarkably, allows the text to speak for itself. In this short book you get a comprehensive and scholarly analysis of what Matthew is saying without getting bogged down in the detail. Not shirking the difficult questions, Storkey uses a light touch, allowing Matthew to illuminate issues facing us today.

Whether you are familiar with Matthew or approaching it for the first time, I can't think of a better book to read on this Gospel. Storkey's inspirational account of Jesus is a fresh invitation to meet him today.'
Andrew Fellows, former Chair of L'Abri Fellowship and Director of L'Abri UK, now Director of Apologetics for Christian Heritage and Pastor at Panton Street Church, Cambridge

'This inspiring and challenging book takes the reader on a deep spiritual journey through the Gospel of Matthew. It contains fascinating historical insights and shows the relevance of Jesus' birth, ministry, death and resurrection for today's world in clear and accessible language.

At the end of each chapter, the helpful questions for reflection make it ideal for home group study at any time, but particularly at Lent. (If a five-week Lent course were needed, one based on Chapters 1, 2, 3, 4 and 6 would work well.)

I am very much looking forward to using it in my own ministry. It will be invaluable as an inspiration for sermon-writing on Matthew's Gospel, as well as a gripping book for home group members. It will also be a key resource for anyone with an interest in finding out more about Jesus.'
The Reverend Claire Robertson, Lordsbridge Team Vicar, Diocese of Ely

Elaine Storkey is a philosopher, sociologist and theologian who has held university posts at King's College London; Stirling; Oxford; Calvin College, USA; and the Open University. A Fellow of Aberystwyth University, high-table member of Newnham College, Cambridge, and former Director of the London Institute for Contemporary Christianity, she has also lectured in Africa, Asia, Canada and Haiti. Her presidency of Tearfund, the aid and development agency, spanned 17 years. A broadcaster and author, she has been a passionate advocate for justice and gender issues for 30 years, implementing many changes for women through 28 years on the General Synod of the Church of England. She presented 'Thought for the Day' on BBC Radio 4 for 20 years and continues to broadcast regularly on *Sunday Sequence*, BBC Radio Ulster. Her writings include *The Search for Intimacy* (Hodder/Eerdmans, 1994) and *The Origins of Difference* (Baker, 2002). Her book *Scars Across Humanity: Understanding and overcoming violence against women* (SPCK, 2015/IVP USA, 2018) won the *Christianity Today* 2019 Book of the Year Award, Politics and Public Life. Her most recent book is *Women in a Patriarchal World* (SPCK, 2020).

MEETING GOD IN MATTHEW

Elaine Storkey

First published in Great Britain in 2022

Society for Promoting Christian Knowledge
36 Causton Street
London SW1P 4ST
www.spck.org.uk

British Library Cataloguing-in-Publication Data
A catalogue record for this book is available from the British Library

ISBN 978-0-281-08195-0
eBook ISBN 978-0-281-08196-7

1 3 5 7 9 10 8 6 4 2

Typeset by Manila Typesetting Company
First printed in Great Britain by Clays Limited
Subsequently digitally printed in Great Britain

eBook by Manila Typesetting Company

Produced on paper from sustainable forests

To

David and Carrie Grant,
who show so much of God's redemptive love

Contents

Acknowledgements

I am grateful to SPCK for the invitation to write this book and it has given me great pleasure to get into the text of Matthew at the depth necessary to share it with others. But even more I am grateful to so many biblical scholars and colleagues who have provided me with many hours of reading and insights, and some invaluable conversations. This is my own work, but the input from others has been incalculable. It would be unwise to name them in case I inadvertently omitted someone. But my debt to many is reflected and acknowledged in the chapters that follow.

As always, I have relied on the support and encouragement of Alan, whose love for the Gospel according to Matthew is as great as my own. It gives him as much pleasure as it gives me to think that this book might be helpful in drawing other people into Matthew's text.

Elaine Storkey
Cambridge 2022

Introduction

Matthew – audience and author

The Gospel according to St Matthew has inspired people for centuries, whether as preachers and Bible students or as musicians and artists. It has had a crucial impact on communities and cultures throughout Christian history. When we consider its message, that is not surprising. In both its beginning and ending the same compelling note is sounded: the assurance that God is present in human life in the person of Jesus. In the very first chapter we're reminded that the name of Jesus is to be 'Emmanuel, God with us'. In the very last chapter Jesus himself tells his disciples, 'And surely I am with you always, to the very end of the age.' From start to conclusion, Matthew's Gospel is centred on Jesus, the Christ, the anointed one of God who, in person or through the Holy Spirit, abides with us.

This Gospel opens the books of the New Testament. That suggests to us straightaway that the earliest Christians saw it as the first account to be written of the life and ministry of Jesus. And indeed it was quoted more than any other Gospel in the second century. But today, few scholars believe that Matthew's Gospel came first and people largely agree that this honour is given to Mark's Gospel, dated around AD 65. The Gospel bearing Matthew's name is widely regarded to be a work compiled later, sometime between AD 67 and AD 85. This dating is said to make more sense of the incidents recorded, the theological undertones and the language and style of writing. It is also said to reflect what was happening in the Jewish Christian community at that time. Whatever date it is given, however, the high estimation of this Gospel's significance remains. Matthew's story of Jesus, his ministry and miracles, his teaching of the kingdom and the demands of Christian discipleship, has left a huge mark on Christian history. His account of Jesus' death and resurrection continues to resonate across the world. Today, as ever before, people meet God in its pages and the Gospel is carried into ever more cultures and communities.

Matthew's Gospel has other credentials that mark it out as distinct from the other Gospels. It is strongly identified as the 'Jewish' Gospel. We recognize the evangelist as an authentic Jewish believer, reaching out to people who share his legacy. Even in the way Matthew structures his account, we can see his desire to engage with those who know the history of the people of Israel and value their heritage.

I shall be looking at this in more detail in the first chapter of this book. Yet this introduction gives an opportunity to raise one issue of Matthew's Jewish background that baffles some readers and poses a dilemma. He clearly sees Jewish law and tradition as highly significant in the life of Jesus, even to the extent of pointing out that Jesus' mission is to the 'lost sheep of the house of Israel' (10.5–6; 15.24). And yet, alongside his own loyalty to the Hebrew Scriptures, he is also controversial. The official representatives of the Jewish religion and state come in for regular criticism, and Matthew's tone towards them can be direct and disparaging, even harsh. For example, he reports

Jesus' warning to the people that unless their 'righteousness surpasses that of the Pharisees and the teachers of the law', they will 'not enter the kingdom of heaven' (5.20). He shows how Jesus criticizes the way leaders put heavy loads on people's shoulders but are unwilling to help them. He castigates Jewish opponents as 'whitewashed tombs', a 'brood of vipers', 'blind guides', 'hypocrites' and 'serpents'. He even lets us know how Jesus praised the faith of a Gentile soldier while denouncing faithlessness in Israel – a sting indeed for law-emphasizing Jews. This deliberate targeting of those in religious authority has led some people to accuse the Gospel writer of being far from pro-Jewish.[1] They point to the statements where Matthew suggests, somewhat darkly, that Israel itself is under judgement by God. And indeed, who can read the cry, 'His blood is on us and on our children' (27.25), without a shiver going up the spine?

This harshness towards their historic community has provoked some Jewish scholars to question the editorship and agenda of this book, doubting that it could ever have been the work of a Jewish writer. Rabbi Michael J. Cook, Professor of Judeo-Christian Studies at Hebrew Union College, stated simply: 'The Gospel according to Matthew has a persistent anti-Jewish animus.'[2] Since Cook was committed to positive Christian–Jewish engagement, this clearly saddened him; it was probably one of the impulses that led to his decision to spend decades teaching New Testament studies to Jewish students.

In response, Christian biblical scholars have looked carefully at Matthew's polemical style in these passages and offered a number of responses. Some see his statements in the line of prophetic tradition, echoing the vehemence of the prophets in the Hebrew Scriptures in holding to account those who claim to speak or judge in the name of God. Some point out that in his passion to confront hypocrisy, the evangelist is as fierce in his denunciations of unfaithful Christians as he is in his criticisms of Jewish influencers (they argue, for example, that a story about an unfaithful servant (24.48–51) is aimed at Christian leaders, not Jews). Others argue that Matthew is highlighting the moral failings of the accepted authorities to heighten our understanding of the integrity of Jesus. (I find this suggestion somewhat unconvincing.) Dick France sees an 'uncomfortable tension' of someone who loves Israel but mourns the painful fact that the majority of his people have failed to respond to God's call to them.[3] And others recognize we have to weigh Matthew's words against the social and religious conditions of the first-century Church.

> Matthew's primary audience is a Jewish–Christian community in conflict and debate with the larger (unbelieving) Jewish community. Both sides, the church and the synagogue, are claiming to be the true people of God. Both claim Israel's Scriptures as their legacy.[4]

This is an accurate reflection of the state of affairs during the last quarter of the first century. It suggests that Matthew's often critical tone reflects internal debates within communities built on the Jewish heritage, rather than an attack on Jewish identity itself.

One New Testament scholar articulates this position well. Graham Stanton believes that for Matthew's community, indeed for much of early Christianity, the relationship between Christianity and Judaism was a central issue for theology and understanding God's will for our lives. By now, the Christian believers had parted company with Judaism, but only after a period of prolonged hostility. The strong language we see in Matthew reflects their ongoing experience of pain and separation. He explains: 'Opposition, rejection and persecution from some Jewish quarters is not just a matter of past experience; for the evangelist and his community the threat is still felt strongly and keenly.'[5] This new Christian minority community was carrying out the commission from Jesus to take the good news to all nations. Yet its members had to do this while struggling with the trauma of separation and the pain of denunciation from their own Jewish kinsfolk.[6] We should not be surprised then to find that the rejection of Jesus by the scribes and Pharisees becomes a focus in the Gospel, and that Matthew's language is strong.

Ronald Clements offers a succinct summary of this crucial period of Jewish–Christian history:

At this time 70–100 CE both Jews and Christians were finding their own individual ways in affirming what was central and essential and what was not. It marked the time when various Christian traditions emerged: e.g. The Epistle to the Hebrews and St John's Gospel. Matthew's Gospel is such a vital witness to this initial period of debate and turmoil which led eventually to the 'parting of the ways' between Jews and Christians. This was not really firmly fixed, however, until the 3rd and 4th centuries when both sides firmly established their individual canons of scripture. For Jews this led to the Mishnah as the new Table of Law, based on Pharisaic principles. For Christians, after Constantine it brought a wide assimilation to the main lines of Hellenistic culture and philosophy and led to the great Councils of 327 CE and 584. After this period only limited debate took place between Jews and Christians.[7]

What is undeniable is that we meet God in Matthew's Gospel through the Hebrew Scriptures and in Jesus. Its roots are unmistakeably Jewish and its vision is Christian.

Who was Matthew?

Sometimes we find it difficult to come to terms with the fact that all the Gospels are anonymous. No one claimed to have written them. Of course, for centuries certain individuals were credited with authorship: Matthew's and John's Gospels were understood to be written by Jesus' apostles of those names. Mark's Gospel was penned by the secretary of St Peter, and Luke's Gospel was the account of 'the beloved physician' who travelled with St Paul (and also authored the Book of Acts). Yet these were attributed a century after the Gospels were written, influenced by key Christian figures like Papias (AD 60–130) and Irenaeus (AD 130–202). Papias declared, 'Matthew put together the oracles [of the Lord] in the Hebrew language and each one interpreted them as best he could.'[8]

Over the past 200 years, various 'schools' of biblical criticism have debated questions of authorship, sources and dating of the Gospels. This is not the place to try to rehearse their arguments and others have done it thoroughly.[9] (The 'two-source hypothesis' will be briefly outlined in Appendix 3.) Disagreements still abound, however, with old theories occasionally enjoying resurgence as new arguments are put forward. Some years ago, New Testament scholar John Wenham looked back wryly at his time in debate on these issues:

> I found myself in the Synoptic Problem Seminar of the Society for New Testament Studies, whose members were in disagreement over every aspect of the subject. When this international group disbanded in 1982 they had sadly to confess that after twelve years' work they had not reached a common mind on a single issue.[10]

Few issues have been finally resolved. Biblical scholar Dick France, in his commentary on Matthew's Gospel written more than 30 years ago, cautions against too hasty a dismissal of the part played in its composition by Matthew the apostle. He also resists a late dating of the Gospel. He points out that nothing in the wording in Matthew suggests that the destruction of the Jerusalem Temple by the Romans (in AD 70) had already taken place, and he challenges the implicit assumption that Jesus could not foresee these as future events. He wonders too why references to temple practices would have been worth making if the Temple had already gone. His conclusion is that 'in the end we simply do not know the role of the apostle Matthew in the composition of the first gospel, but the tradition of the early church encourages us to believe that it was a major one'.[11]

Writing around 20 years after Dick France, Richard Bauckham mounts a case for the importance of the eyewitness tradition in compiling the Gospels. He argues that although Matthew the apostle was unlikely to have been the one who wrote down the first Gospel, he was clearly an eyewitness to much of Christ's ministry, and the reason the Gospel was attributed to him may well have been that his own testimonies played a significant role in its content.[12] Popular author Steve Hays cites the many Jewish attributes of Matthew the disciple and believes 'the apostle Matthew is an unlikely candidate for a mistaken or fabricated authorship attribution'. He feels it unlikely also that the author would have been universally unknown in all the extant sources 'if he was somebody other than Matthew'.[13]

Nevertheless, even though there is considerable confidence among scholars in dating Matthew's Gospel after that of Mark, and in analysing the overlapping material among Matthew, Mark and Luke, difficulties over authorship remain. The later the dating, the more likely it is to be someone other than the apostle. So, apart from being reasonably sure that he was a well-taught Jew within an early Jewish-Christian community, we can have no further certainty about his identity or his link with the apostle of that name.

Matthew in art and music

The fact that we cannot be certain of the identity of the Gospel writer has not deterred the imagination of people who have found him a significant subject for their art. What the evangelist might have looked like has inspired painters throughout the centuries. Hundreds of traditional icons have depicted him typically with flowing beard, holding the Scriptures in one hand while turning the pages with the other. The sumptuous colours, golden halos, pious expressions have all attempted to represent the 'sacred' and draw away from everyday thoughts and pursuits into meditation and worship.

Later artists have portrayed him less stylistically, their art often making implicit theological statements. Paintings are frequently of Matthew the human author, aided by an angel to write under the inspiration and authority of God. Caravaggio's painting, *The Inspiration of Saint Matthew* (1602), is particularly dramatic. A swirling angel confronts and startles Matthew at work as he turns from his writing to receive the revelation. The angel's dynamic entrance, the multiple circles forming two powerful points of light in the darkness, the depths of colour all convey the dramatic seriousness of being a harbinger of truth from God. Frans Hals' *St Matthew* (1625) shows a deeply contemplative, bearded Matthew, holding open Scriptures that take up almost a quarter of the canvas, and from which light emanates in the darkness; he carefully reads the text, while the childlike face of a young angel looks up through the darkness to offer encouragement. Rembrandt's work, *St Matthew and the Angel* (c. 1661), offers us an exquisite gentle rugged portrait of a pensive, thoughtful, elderly Matthew, with pen poised and listening intently as the angel behind him whispers words of divine inspiration; God's golden light in the darkness is reflected on both their faces and on God's word.

Musicians have also been captivated by the work of the evangelist and inspired by his text to bring the good news of the Gospel to the people who need to hear it. J. S. Bach's powerful, moving oratorio, *St Matthew Passion*, takes us through the last days of Christ's life, as recounted in chapters 26 and 27 of Matthew's Gospel. The music is captivating in its extraordinary range of voices and emotions, as Bach offers us multiple layers of musical meaning. Even though it is an oratorio, the composer wanted everyone to participate in the worship, so included a number of hymn-like chorales within the solo section. The beautiful *'Erkenne mich, mein Hüter'* (Recognize me, my guardian) is repeated throughout the oratorio and draws the whole audience into a spiritual experience as they sing and reflect on Matthew's account of Jesus' Passion.

Through Matthew's Gospel, musicians and artists have been drawn to meet God. Their encounter with the text has inspired them to put colour on canvas and notes on a score to express in artistic creativity their own awe for the biblical narrative.

It is time now for us to search the Gospel to see for ourselves what is revealed there, and allow Matthew to take us into the good news of Jesus. So, please join me on a journey through Matthew's text. My suggestion is that you have the Bible open at the relevant chapters in Matthew as you read this book so you can follow up the many references for yourself and receive what the evangelist brings to your heart through God's Holy Spirit.

1

Meeting God in fulfilment of prophecy

The 'Jewish' Gospel

I was taken aback when a Jewish friend once told me that I would never understand Matthew's Gospel without getting to grips with the way Jewish people think. It was a teasing observation rather than a rebuke. My surprise was linked to the fact that I felt, naively, that the Gospel somehow 'belonged' to me, as a Christian, rather than to a practising Jew! As the years have gone on, I have begun to understand more what he meant.

As the author of the 'Jewish' Gospel, Matthew did know how Jewish people thought, and he addressed his readers in ways that spoke clearly into their background. All the way through, his writing makes copious references to the Hebrew Scriptures. This is not in itself unique, for quotations and allusions to the Old Testament occur in all the Gospels, but in this Gospel the pattern is most pronounced. In fact, he quotes the Old Testament around 65 times, more than twice as many times as Mark. Sometimes Matthew gives us a standard translation of the Hebrew text, but also translates it more freely and independently with the confidence of one at home with the biblical authors. In other places, Matthew simply makes allusions to the Old Testament without quoting any specific book or passage. He refers regularly both to the Torah and to the prophetic writers, and also affirms that Jesus has fulfilled the Law and the Prophets (5.17).

What becomes evident from the very beginning is that Matthew's comfortable familiarity with the Hebrew Scriptures and his freedom to draw on prophecies and passages is aimed at making the gospel specifically relevant to his readers.

Matthew also draws on Jewish culture and customs. Again, we find this in the other Gospels, but with different nuances in Matthew. He seems to take for granted that readers will understand the references without him having to labour the point or give the further explanations offered by Luke or John. For example, ceremonial handwashing (15.2), the temple tax (17.24–27), using phylacteries and tassels (23.5) and 'whitewashed tombs' (23.27) are all referred to without any further ado. He mentions 'the temple' some 17 times in the Gospel without feeling the need to add 'in Jerusalem'. It is clear to him that his readers will recognize immediately which temple he is referring to. The differences in the phrases used by Matthew from those in the other Gospels also suggest that he is concerned about Jewish sensitivities. Many commentators mention that he is the only Gospel author to speak of the 'kingdom of heaven' rather than the 'kingdom of God'.

Meeting God in the Hebrew Scriptures is a complex business. It is not simply a task for scholarship. It is a task for living. Biblical authors, in both testaments, aim pointed criticisms at those who know the Law and the Prophets in detail, yet are spiritually indifferent to what God tells us through their teaching. Matthew's involvement in Scripture shows something very different. The Gospel attributed to him discloses an intimate, spiritual relationship with both the text and the spirit of the Hebrew Bible. His is a deep heart-knowledge rather than simply one of intellect. His purpose is to draw his readers into a deeper encounter with God through Jesus.

The Old Testament writers wrote to readers who wanted to know God better through his word. God spoke through the prophet Jeremiah about the covenant relation between God and God's people: 'I will put my law within them, and I will write it on their hearts; and I will be their God and they shall be my people' (Jeremiah 31.33, NRSV). The psalmist also acknowledged his desire to be led by God through the Scriptures: 'Your word is a lamp for my feet, a light on my path' (Psalm 119.105). 'Belief' for the faithful Hebrew reader did not mean 'intellectual assent' to a set of propositions; faith was neither a leap into the unknown nor (merely) an acceptance of reasoned arguments. It was simply obedience to God through the Law's requirements and the Prophets' directions. Matthew's use of biblical references is an active, engaged response. It echoes the aspiration of all committed believers to be guided by God's word.

The honest transparency of the psalmist is echoed in the Gospel of Matthew, especially his prayer: 'Search me, God, and know my heart; test me and know my anxious thoughts. See if there is any offensive way in me, and lead me in the way everlasting' (Psalm 139.23–24). Matthew knew that those who gladly received God's revelation would understand its demands for integrity in their lives. In inviting us into the story of Jesus' life, Matthew wants us to take it into our hearts and let it impact our lives.

Matthew's aim, then, was to delve into the Hebrew Scriptures to show those who respected and were schooled in them that their Scriptures pointed to Jesus. It's a process we find documented in other parts of the New Testament. After the resurrection, Jesus took his followers on the road to Emmaus through the books of Moses and the Prophets so they could understand that the Messiah had to suffer and enter his glory (Luke 24.25–27). When Philip was suddenly led from Jerusalem to the Ethiopian eunuch on the way to Gaza, he opened up Isaiah's prophecy of the lamb led to the slaughter so that the Ethiopian would know its fulfilment in Jesus (Acts 8.34–35). When Paul and Barnabas went to Salamis and Antioch they unpacked the Hebrew Scriptures to Jewish worshippers in the synagogues so they could see Jesus as the continuation and fulfilment of their historic biblical storyline (Acts 13). God's revelation in the Old Testament spoke to them all as first-century believers and led them to the completion of God's fulfilment in Jesus.

The genealogy (Matthew 1)

When we begin to read the Gospel of Matthew we can be somewhat baffled by the way it starts. We may find ourselves immediately distanced from its narrative. Since we're all familiar with the story of the baby in the manger heralded by angelic voices and visiting shepherds, we might expect the first Gospel in the New Testament to open with an account of Jesus' birth. But Matthew begins with a genealogy. He takes us through a roll-call of 14 generations that preceded Jesus. This is entirely in keeping with all we have just noted about the links with the Hebrew Scriptures, but it feels odd in our culture. It's not the normal way we invite someone into a spiritual encounter! It's obvious why. A lengthy list of ancestors, peppered with names like Amminadab, Sheal-tiel and Zerubbabel leaping over centuries, hardly offers the most inspiring route for a meeting with God; it would more likely be a massive turn-off.

Yet for Matthew's audience it was crucial. Biblical scholar Jeffrey Siker reflects on what this meant to his readers compared with those in our contemporary world:

> While Western cultures tend to have little interest in genealogies, viewing them as tedious curiosities, Matthew and his readers would have considered this announcement to be the most exciting news of all time. The genealogy introduces Jesus as the 'son of Abraham' and the 'son of David,' meaning he is in the lineage of two of the most significant figures in biblical history.[1]

The process is intentional. Matthew is assembling the genealogy of the one who is the Messiah, God's chosen one in Jewish history. His aim is to identify Jesus from the very beginning of his account, before he reports a single word spoken or miracle performed. So how does he do that?

The genealogy fulfils at least five key functions. It designates Jesus from the outset as a Jew. It traces him back to Abraham. It locates his royal descent through the tribe of Judah, staking his right to the title 'King of the Jews'. It cites Ruth as an ancestor and so establishes Jesus as the 'son of David'. It presents his heritage through three historical phases of 14 generations, indicating that the time of fulfilment has come.

It does not matter that Matthew abridges the genealogy in producing these three groups of generations (from Abraham to David, from David to the captivity and from the captivity to the birth of Christ). His Jewish readers will not be quibbling about his simplifying of their history or his patterning it in this way; the teaching methods often employed by the rabbis were designed to make it easy for people to remember. The main thing is that in naming Jesus the son of Abraham and the son of David, Matthew knows that his readers will understand the implications. They will know that God made a covenant with Abraham, promising he would create through him a great nation through whose descendants all the nations of the earth would be blessed (Genesis 22.17–18). They will know that God also made a covenant with King David, promising him that one of his descendants would reign on his throne for ever (2 Samuel 7.11–16). They will also know the story of the exile and the people's emptiness in their experience of absence from Jerusalem. They will know the promise of the Messiah. In relating Jesus' genealogy, Matthew places the coming of Christ so clearly in the long story of Israel.

Yet there is still something vaguely baffling about this particular genealogy, and that is Matthew's choice of ancestral names. Genealogies do bring something of a risk. Many people today researching their family tree discover people whose lives weren't all that exemplary. A friend of mine was somewhat dismayed to learn that one of her predecessors had spent years in prison for corruption. When we look at the individuals named by Matthew in the genealogy of Jesus, we might have a similar reaction. He had plenty to choose from, some of whom were very faithful servants of God. So why would he choose Jacob who stole his brother's blessing, Judah who sold his brother into slavery and 12 ancestral kings (out of a list of 14) who were 'an odd assortment of adulterers, murderers, incompetents, power-seekers, and harem-wastrels'?[2] Even the women he mentions were not the esteemed wives of the patriarchs – Sarah, Rebecca and Rachel – but Tamar, the Canaanite woman who disguised herself as a prostitute to seduce Judah, and Rahab, a prostitute who hid Joshua and his friends. And did you notice the woman, unnamed, who had been sexually exploited? When Matthew tells us that 'David was the father of Solomon, whose mother had been Uriah's wife' (1.6), he seems to be subtly (though quite definitely) pointing to David's adultery and seduction (or rape?) of Bathsheba and the murder of Bathsheba's husband. Even respected kings were no paragons of virtue. This motley crew were all offered as people in the genealogical history of Jesus. Author Ronald Rolheiser summarizes:

What Matthew reveals in his list of people begetting other people is . . . quite a checkered story. Jesus' family tree contains as many sinners as saints and his origins take their roots too in the crooked lines written by liars, betrayers, adulterers, and murderers. Jesus was pure, but his origins were not.[3]

So, given the availability of names for his ancestral account, we might well ask why Matthew selected those. It may be that he was prompted by the Holy Spirit to show us something unexpected about God. We might meet the God who did not fulfil his promises through people because of their righteousness, but in spite of their sin. And we might learn too that God's plans 'aren't derailed by our infidelities, sin and scheming' as his purposes still come to pass.[4]

But it could also be that Matthew lets us see the implications of all this for our own personal lives. Jesus' generational history confirms that God's grace can work through any of us, whatever our past or present, and bring his purposes to fruition. This list of forebears brings us face to face with the fact that the God we meet in Matthew is not a God who blesses us because of our impeccable ancestral heritage or our devout grandparents. We are blessed because of God's own love for us, whoever we are and whatever our background.

The realization that God calls us out of any context deepens our understanding of God's power over our former lives. If our past is one we regret, we can face it with God, knowing that we can be forgiven for any sins we have committed in it. If our personal history is so damaged that we feel crippled by it and wake in the night with memories that hurt, God is the one who can release and heal us. The past does matter, but it need never have the final word. God's love can bind up our wounds, restore our spirit and send us out in freedom with renewed steps.

So, although the genealogy was to reassure Matthew's Jewish contemporaries, it can also lift our spirits today. It can remind us, as Rolheiser wisely observes, that 'the God who wrote the beginning with crooked lines also writes the sequence with crooked lines, and some of those lines are our own lives and witness'.[5] Even more, it helps us see that no one needs to live with the failure of the past when Jesus offers us peace for the present and hope for the future.

The Nativity (Matthew 1 – 2)

When we move from the genealogy to Matthew's account of the Nativity, we find it nothing like as detailed as Luke's. He tells us nothing of the dramatic annunciation to Mary, the census, the crowded inns, the chorus of angels and the shepherds coming to visit the Christ child. The main character in Matthew's narrative is Joseph not Mary (possibly following the central Jewish assumption of the time that the central representative of a household is the husband/ father). And the visit of the wise men is found in this Gospel alone. What is more, Old Testament references actually make up more than half the text in the chronicle of Jesus' birth. Those references don't develop the story, however, and if we removed them, we would still be left with a perfectly coherent narrative. Matthew's account of Mary's unexpected pregnancy, Joseph's visit from the angel, the birth of Jesus, the coming of the Magi, the fleeing to Egypt and the new family settling in Galilee would all stay intact. So what, then, does Matthew add here by his many references to the Hebrew Scriptures?

9

Glenn Pemberton is quick to provide an answer. He suggests that, quite simply, they provide the point of the Gospel: 'Matthew's *story* is not damaged by excluding his Old Testament references. However, Matthew's *message* about Jesus is decimated by such exclusion.'[6] Pemberton argues that something so essential is provided to this Gospel by the Old Testament citations, that if we fail to engage with them or understand how Matthew is using them, we will simply fail to grasp the Gospel's underlying purpose or meaning. Once again, Matthew is opening up the Hebrew Scriptures to those who already know them, so they will recognize that the Scriptures point to Jesus.

The version of the Nativity presented to us by Matthew is not only shorter than Luke's, but also recounted from a different angle. It is less of an account of the actual birth of Jesus than one of his origin, name and link with prophecy. It serves to establish Jesus' legal lineage and emphasizes the virgin birth. When the angel appears in a dream to Joseph with news of the pregnancy, the words he uses somewhat curiously echo those of the angel visiting Hagar in the desert telling her she will give birth (Genesis 16.11). We are told of Joseph's surprise at Mary's pregnancy, knowing the child is not his, which gives greater weight to the idea of a divine conception. Yet Matthew quotes from Isaiah (7.14), not simply to prove the virgin birth, but to emphasize that the child will be called 'Immanuel', adding his own translation: 'God with us' (1.23). Matthew is clearly conveying that the subject of his biography is not simply a charismatic rabbinic healer who could draw the crowds. His genealogy, birth and prophetic significance disclose that he is nothing less than the Anointed One of God, the Christ, the Saviour of the world. The baby born in Bethlehem and worshipped by wise men from the East is indeed 'the focal point and destination of human history'.[7]

Prophecy and its fulfilment

When Matthew refers to the virgin birth of Jesus (1.22–23) *fulfilling* the prophecy of Isaiah 7.14, he is deliberately drawing on the prophetic tradition and beginning a process that recurs throughout the Gospel. He draws us into meeting God in God's covenantal faithfulness and in the promises made through the prophets despite the waywardness of God's people. The promise-fulfilment theme is a key one in the Gospel, taken up and developed in five sections of Matthew's Gospel, each of them starting with a 'fulfilment quotation'. The form each time is similar. We are given an announcement about an event, followed by terminology (unique to Matthew) something like 'this was to fulfil what God said through the prophet', and then a reference to a prophecy in the Hebrew Scriptures. In this way, Matthew claims that the birth of Jesus by the virgin (1.22–23) fulfils the prophecy of Isaiah 7.14; Joseph's fleeing with his family to Egypt (2.14) fulfils Hosea 11.1; the slaughter of the infants by Herod fulfils Jeremiah 31.15; and Jesus' ministry in Galilee (4.14–16) fulfils Isaiah 9.2.

Yet what does Matthew mean by 'fulfilment'? It's an important question because it doesn't always fit our expectations. We often think of fulfilment as a one-to-one relation between prediction and something happening, along the lines of 'this is what the prophet predicted about the Messiah, and here's what happened hundreds of years later, which fulfilled it'. And we certainly do read prophecies in Matthew that conform somewhat to this pattern. Take the famous passage in Isaiah 9.2, 6–9:

The people who walked in darkness
Have seen a great light;
Those who dwelt in the land of the shadow of death,
Upon them a light has shined.

For unto us a Child is born,
Unto us a Son is given;
And the government will be upon His shoulder.
And His name will be called
Wonderful, Counselor, Mighty God,
Everlasting Father, Prince of Peace.
Of the increase of His government and peace
There will be no end,
Upon the throne of David and over His kingdom,
To order it and establish it with judgment and justice
From that time forward, even forever.
The zeal of the Lord of hosts will perform this.
(NKJV)

This is a wonderfully predictive prophecy, set to powerful music by Handel in *The Messiah*. It is very satisfying to see its 'fulfilment' in the very person of Jesus, beginning with his birth and continuing through his ministry. Because the link here is so evident between prophecy and fulfilment, we assume the same clarity can be seen in all Matthew's references to Old Testament prophecies. Yet we would be wrong. It might seem strange to us, but Matthew does not often choose obviously 'predictive' prophecies. And when he quotes Isaiah 9, it is not to focus on the promise of the child, fulfilled by Jesus' birth (vv. 6–9), but on the shining of God's light on people, fulfilled by his ministry (v. 2).

Thousands of scholarly words have examined Matthew's use of Old Testament prophecy, so it is worth taking a little time here trying to tease it out more ourselves. Let's start in the first chapter, when the angel comes to reassure Joseph that Mary has not been unfaithful to him but has had a miraculous conception from the Holy Spirit:

'She will give birth to a son, and you are to give him the name Jesus, because he will save his people from their sins.' All this took place to fulfil what the Lord had said through the prophet: 'The virgin will conceive and give birth to a son, and they will call him Immanuel' (which means 'God with us').
(1.20–23)

We assume that Matthew's reference to Isaiah's prophecy in 7.1–17 is a prediction of the birth of the Messiah. Yet when we go into the passage we find the prophecy relates to Ahaz, the idolatrous king of Judah, whom God is promising to help deliver the people from Ahaz's enemies, despite his treachery. God gives him a sign – the conception, birth and naming of a child (Isaiah 7.13–14). And that prophecy was fulfilled hundreds of years earlier. So, what do we make of this? How is it relevant to Joseph's visit from an angel? Some sceptics even accuse Matthew of simply lifting an Old Testament passage because it suits his purposes.

Yet it's much more meaningful than that. We recognize that Isaiah's prophecy is effectively being fulfilled in two stages. It is first fulfilled in the way Isaiah predicts: God saves the people of Judah, despite Ahaz's disobedience, and the warring kings do not overcome them. The child born then is a sign of God's ongoing mercy and protection. But because the prophecy was fulfilled then, it doesn't mean that is the end of it. A second fulfilment might not even have been envisaged by Isaiah, but that does not stop the Holy Spirit from continuing to speak through him. As Wenham points out, 'The Holy Spirit knew beforehand the course of history with its consummation in Christ and so in guiding the writers he intended a deeper meaning than they understood.'[8] So the Holy Spirit is telling us through Isaiah that, hundreds of years into the future, another child will be born to a virgin mother and this child will save the people from their sins. He will be called Immanuel, confirming that God is indeed with his people. Rather than accusing Matthew of 'lifting' an Old Testament passage out of context, we can recognize its deep prophetic meaning through history for his own times. Prophecy is often intricate, pointing to different events and yielding layers of meaning.

This complexity is even more evident in Matthew's 'fulfilment quotation' in the next chapter, following the visit of the wise men (2.14–15). The angel comes to warn Joseph of the impending danger from Herod. Matthew tells us that Joseph gets up, takes the child and his mother during the night and leaves for Egypt, where they stay until Herod dies. Matthew comments: 'This was to fulfil what had been spoken by the Lord through the prophet, "Out of Egypt I have called my son"' (NRSV). Yet, once again, when we look at the Old Testament reference in Hosea, we can be puzzled by what we find. We see straight away that it is not a predictive prophecy about the flight from Egypt by Joseph and his family. In fact, it is not a prophecy at all. It is a statement recalling something in the past. Through Hosea, God declares his love for Israel, remembers that he called them out from Egypt, and is considering how to deal with them now. John Goldingay sums it up well:

Hosea 11 is a record of God's inner wrestling over whether he is to act in relation to Israel with love or with judgment. It opens by recalling the blessings God had given to his people – beginning with his calling them out of Egypt at the time of the exodus. Thus Hosea 11:1 is not prophecy (in the sense of a statement about the future, which could thus be capable of being 'fulfilled') at all. It is history.[9]

Matthew sees in the text what Hosea saw, but also hears something bigger. He hears how those distant events that occur and reoccur in the story of Israel echo loudly in the life of Jesus. Matthew develops an Israel–Jesus typology throughout his Gospel and it applies here. Just as God brought his 'son' Israel out of Egypt, so Jesus, God's Son, is also brought out of Egypt. Just as Israel was tested for 40 years in the desert, so Jesus is tested by Satan for 40 days in the wilderness. But the contrasts are highly significant. Israel's release from Egyptian bondage did not draw the people to greater love for God and a desire for committed service. In fact, they failed badly. They courted idolatry, built a golden calf, hardened their hearts, complained and railed against God; they even wandered aimlessly in the wilderness for 40 years. Most of those called out of Egypt never even entered the promised land. But God's Son Jesus shows something very different. In his life, teaching, obedience and love he fulfils the messianic hope of deliverance and brings God's compassion to all who would in repentance receive it. In short, while Israel repeatedly failed to obey God, Jesus, the new Israel, remained faithful, fulfilling all that had been hoped for in being brought out of Egypt.

We begin to see what Matthew is doing in these two, and many other, fulfilment quotations. It is not proof-texting. He is not saying: 'Look, this is what the prophets said the Messiah would be (or do, or be part of); lo and behold, this is exactly what happened!' It's not a case of showing events, situations and actions predicted of the Messiah, and pointing out that Jesus is doing them. In some of the prophecies, prediction does take this form, but not here. Often, Old Testament passages cited by Matthew make no overt claims about the coming of the Messiah; they are prophecies or narratives where God's purposes were not completely fulfilled at the time. Matthew, in this chapter and elsewhere, is telling us that those purposes are being completed or fulfilled now through Jesus. Dick France observes the deep, rich nature of Matthew's appeal to the Hebrew Scriptures and says he was 'deliberately composing a chapter rich in potential exegetical bonuses, so that the more fully a reader shared the religious traditions and scriptural erudition of the author, the more he was likely to derive from his reading'.[10] So there are clear surface meanings and deeper bonus meanings that lead us to the person and role of the Messiah.

We realize, then, that the significance of texts can exceed the immediate meaning recognized by the Old Testament prophet, but still be intended by God and imparted by the Holy Spirit. This helps us to understand 'fulfilment' in a richer way.[11] We've already seen that it can convey the sense of contrast, where Jesus fulfils what God's people did not – in fact they often broke their covenantal relationship with God. It can also convey the sense of completeness, where Jesus filled to overflowing the unfinished business implied in the quoted Scripture.

Another use has the sense of Jesus fulfilling all righteousness in fulfilling the requirements of the Law and the Prophets (5.17), as Jesus said he had come to do. Many of Matthew's fulfilment quotations are infused with the concept of God's redemptive purpose in human history, so we should not be surprised to find Matthew looking at the previous salvation history of God's people and the way Jesus is bringing that to completion. In all these ways, Matthew helps us to meet God and deepen our relationship when we study his use of prophecy.

I want to finish this discussion of the fulfilment quotations on an easier note. Because we do also have some very straightforward examples of Matthew's use of prophecy that meet all the expectations of prediction. We have already touched on Isaiah 9 and the promise that a child will be born, a son given, and the government will be on his shoulders. But there are more. We have a very clear example early in the Gospel, in connection with the visit of the wise men to Jerusalem. The question is where the Anointed One would be born. Matthew, in 2.6, cites Micah 5.2:

And you, Bethlehem, in the land of Judah,
    are by no means least among the rulers of
      Judah;
    for from you shall come a ruler
    who is to shepherd my people Israel.

This is clearly a predictive prophecy from Micah and was widely accepted as foretelling the birthplace of the future king. What makes the prophecy remarkable is that it identifies the place not to be Jerusalem, as the wise men discovered. Early Jewish interpreters understood this passage to refer to the Messiah, and we can see that the prophecy was fulfilled in the birth of Jesus in Bethlehem. However, the whimsical, almost amusing, fact is how Matthew introduces this into the story. He doesn't quote it as one of his fulfilment prophecies to substantiate the identity of Jesus. It is a dialogue in the narrative of the visit of the wise men. It is, in fact, what the chief priests and scribes confirmed about the birth of the Messiah when they were consulted by Herod! Matthew must have enjoyed the fact that he did not have to provide his own prophetic reference here, as it was done for him by others. He must have enjoyed even more that it was provided for him by the very group of people who would constantly challenge Jesus' messiahship during the years of his ministry. So Matthew does not shirk from using the insights of the religious establishment when they 'inadvertently' confirm the message of his Gospel!

It's interesting to look at a few of the other prophecies quoted by Matthew that share this directness. For example, in chapter 8 Jesus carries out healings and exorcisms, and Matthew points us to Isaiah 53.4: 'this was to fulfil what had been spoken through the prophet Isaiah, "He took our infirmities and bore our diseases"' (8.17, NRSV). In chapter 12, Jesus' gentle ministry and refusal of the limelight prompts Matthew to quote one of the Servant Songs in Isaiah 42: 'Here is my servant, whom I have chosen, my beloved, with whom my soul is well pleased . . . He will not break a bruised reed or quench a smouldering wick until he brings justice to victory' (12.18, 20, NRSV). In chapter 13, Jesus himself explains his use of parables in teaching by claiming it is a fulfilment of Psalm 78.2: 'I will open my mouth to speak in parables; I will proclaim what has been hidden from the foundation of the world' (13.35, NRSV). And in chapter 21.4–5, when Jesus rides into Jerusalem on the back of a donkey, Matthew says that was to fulfil what was spoken through the prophet in Zechariah 9.9: 'Tell the daughter of Zion, Look, your king is coming to you, humble, and mounted on a donkey, on a colt, the foal of a donkey'.

Through these and so many more references, the Gospel reveals an author who understands the prophets and loves to share their wisdom and Spirit-given discernment. We are also helped to see for ourselves that Jesus' life and ministry are a crucial focal point of Old Testament prophecy and the culmination of Israel's history.

Jesus' own relation with the Hebrew Scriptures

We have been looking mostly at Matthew's use of the Old Testament in referencing his narrative about Jesus. But he documents many occasions when Jesus himself quotes from the Hebrew Scriptures. This was an integral part of his language and teaching. Jesus drew on all three major sections of the Hebrew Bible: the Law, the Prophets, and the Writings; he knew the Torah intimately and referred to many of the laws, whether moral, civil or ceremonial. For him the biblical writings were authoritative, the word of his Father, for both his audience, and himself and his disciples (John 10.35).

Jesus also referred regularly to the Old Testament narratives to illustrate his teaching, citing key biblical characters as examples of good and bad living. For instance, he encouraged his disciples to face opposition and persecution by reminding them that God's prophets were persecuted in past times (5.11–12). He named Tyre, Sidon and Sodom as paradigms of ancient evil cities and used their fate as a warning to the towns that rejected his teaching from God (11.21–24). He paralleled the three days that Jonah spent in the belly of the whale with the three days Jesus would spend in the tomb (12.40). He referred to the Queen of Sheba, who received wisdom from Solomon, condemning his generation at the judgement, for they could have learned from someone 'greater than Solomon' (12.42). He mentioned Moses, who gave the right for men to divorce as a concession to the hardness of their hearts (19.7–9). He quoted Psalm 8 at the chief priests and scribes when they objected to the children crying

'Hosanna' and praising him in the Temple. He summarized the Ten Commandments to the Pharisees when they ask him which was the greatest commandment (22.35–40). And he referred back to the days of Noah and the catastrophic destruction that occurred when people did not heed the warnings God had given (24.37–39).

The Hebrew Scriptures were not simply the foundation of Jesus' teaching. Most crucially, he acknowledged that they spoke about him, both through the prophets and through Israel's narrative. His powerful parable of the wicked tenants (21.33–45) sketches allegorically Israel's rejection of God's authority, their persecution of the prophets and the killing of God's Son. But he promises there will be judgement. The tenancy will be taken away from them and given to others. He refers his listeners back to Psalm 118.2 in verse 42: 'The stone that the builders rejected has become the cornerstone; this was the Lord's doing and it is amazing in our eyes.' Jesus saw himself as the keystone, the one around whom everything should be put in place, the one in whom, in the words of Paul in Colossians 1.17, 'all things hold together'. The chief priests and Pharisees knew who they were in Jesus' narrative. But Matthew tells us that, rather than seeking help, they plotted to silence him. With the irony of human free will in the course of history, their own decision would make the prophecy fit. Matthew, evangelist and student, was following his Teacher in recognizing Jesus' central role in Jewish and human history.

We acknowledge today that God speaks to us in the Hebrew Scriptures whether through the law, history, prophecy, psalms, dreams, proverbs or even a love song. And we come reverently to those Scriptures to meet God, as people have been doing for centuries. But, as Matthew shows us, when our eyes and hearts are open, we meet him there also in the Anointed One, Messiah, to whom the Scriptures give testimony and witness that he is God's Son.

2

Meeting God in preparation for ministry

Matthew offers us a graphic account of the preparation Jesus underwent before he began his ministry around the age of 30 (Luke 1). For even though he was beyond the early flush of youth, it was not something he immediately threw himself into. The transition from working, presumably as a carpenter, to travelling from town to town to preach the kingdom of heaven had to be thoroughly prepared for. Everything had to be undertaken seeking the Father's guidance and leading. It's a salutary reminder to any of us facing key changes in our lives. The work ethos of today often means we are expected to be ready instantly to create a great impression and hit the ground running. If Jesus needed to take time out to reflect and prepare for the next phase of his calling before God, we may find we need to do this even more.

Matthew notes four distinct aspects of Jesus' preparation that are somewhat different from ones we might take on. These were not simply periods of reflection and examination for Jesus himself, but preparation for others too, especially those he was coming to serve. The first task was to get the ground ready. Members of the Jewish community had to be ready to hear Jesus so that they might quickly begin to realize who he was and what he had come for. The second task was for Jesus to undergo his own act of commitment in baptism. Far more than any ritual, it would be an indication that he was ready to accept the ministry he had come to fulfil and know God's anointing on it. The third phase was a period of intense fasting and isolation, where Jesus would encounter, alone, the spiritual challenges that could test both his faith and his resolve. Fourth and final was the reaching-out phase, where he would choose people to work alongside him and be mentored as his disciples. They too would need to leave their current occupations and 'forsake everything' to follow Jesus.

Each aspect of preparation brought different challenges for those involved, but each was necessary for the fulfilment of Jesus' mission. These periods of preparation were specific to Jesus and for a ministry like no other. Yet they do raise questions for us in our own society, especially for those of us who experience God's calling on our lives, because the current pervading cultural ethos is far less about commitment and more about living according to our own preferences. And when we move into Christian service we sometimes have to disentangle the two.

Jesus did not undertake everything on his own, and Matthew quickly introduces us to someone who played a key part in the first two phases of preparation. John the Baptist was the one chosen to prepare the ground and preach the kingdom in anticipation of the coming Messiah. He was a unique figure in the New Testament whose significance is not always fully recognized, so I want us to look at how Matthew presents this enigmatic person.

John the Baptist (Matthew 3, 11, 14)

John the Baptist is mentioned in all four Gospels. He prepared the way for Jesus, took on the might of the religious authorities and died an awful death. But the Gospel writers are not the only ones who note his significance. The celebrated Jewish historian Flavius Josephus, born in AD 37, mentions him in his very significant work *Antiquities of the Jews* (AD 90). Josephus wrote of John as a 'good man' who 'commanded the Jews to exercise virtue, both as to righteousness towards one another and piety towards God and so come to baptism'. In his opinion John's strong following also posed a threat to King Herod, as well as to the Roman occupiers; insurrection was always possible with someone who had such an impact on Jewish audiences. Josephus writes that they 'came in crowds about him, for they were very greatly moved by his words'.[1] He even feels that this supposed threat to Herod contributed to his death. Josephus is always a writer worth reading. His 'outsider's view' on John, as well as his comments on other people we know from Scripture, gives us a tingling sense of authentic history.

Biblical sources on John help us build up a fuller and more detailed picture. Matthew dedicates a whole chapter to introducing this strange and charismatic leader, and we immediately get a remarkably vivid sketch of John's hermit lifestyle. We learn what he looked like, what he wore and even what he ate. Matthew isn't always interested in these details, so John's camel-haired clothes must have been out of the ordinary. We also get a good sense of John's personality, conveyed in his indifference towards popularity and a refusal to mince his words. As John's story continues through the Gospel, we are forced to agree that his was indeed a 'voice crying in the wilderness'. Yet, as Josephus had also noted, it was a voice that others heeded.

It is not Matthew but Luke who gives us the first glimpse of the relationship between John and Jesus. Luke relates details of the meeting between the pregnant Mary, mother of Jesus, and her cousin Elizabeth, who was also expecting a baby. At the sound of Mary's voice, John the unborn foetus leapt for joy in Elizabeth's womb because of the baby she was carrying (Luke 1.41). Suddenly filled with the Holy Spirit, Elizabeth herself became prophetic: 'But why am I so favoured, that the mother of my Lord should come to me?' It is all a level higher than the experience of a kicking baby enjoyed by most pregnant women! We can see this striking incident as indicating that John met God while in his mother's womb, and this symbolized what was to be the continuing relationship between John and Jesus. John recognized the one who had come as Saviour, and he was to prepare his way. Jesus in turn accepted God's revelation through his cousin and built on it in his own teaching. Though the incident in Luke is not related by Matthew, the same message is conveyed. The accounts of John's public ministry in Matthew's Gospel leave us in no doubt as to his deep spiritual and theological significance.

For a start, it is evident that John the Baptist provided a key bridge between the Old and New Testaments. Though his early years were spent in obscurity, alone in the desert, when he finally emerged as a public preacher his prophetic ministry broke a long silence. The last of the prophets of the Hebrew Scriptures had spoken some 400 years before. Now John was to take up their tradition. Characteristically, Matthew quotes Isaiah about this messenger who was to come to 'prepare the way for the Lord, make straight paths for him' (3.3). He identifies John the Baptist as the one whom Isaiah foresaw. Matthew knew the reference would have special significance for the people of his day, for they knew Isaiah's prophecy. They also knew the prophecy of Malachi, that the messenger who would come before the Messiah was the prophet Elijah, returning to the people. Elijah, the early prophet of Israel, did not undergo a bodily death, according to 2 Kings 2.3–9, but was taken up in a whirlwind.

> See, I will send the prophet Elijah to you before that great and dreadful day of the LORD comes. He will turn the hearts of the parents to their children, and the hearts of the children to their parents; or else I will come and strike the land with total destruction.
> (Malachi 4.5–6)

It is evident from the Gospels that people wanted to know if John was in fact the returning prophet Elijah. Matthew mentions that Elijah does return, to be present at the transfiguration of Jesus as a symbol of the prophets, along with Moses who represents the Law (17.3–4). Jesus also mentions in passing that Elijah has already returned and been ignored. Yet in the Isaiah prophecy (Isaiah 40.3) Elijah is not mentioned by name and Matthew does not identify John as Elijah. It is clear from all the Gospels that John the Baptist is not any literal reincarnation of the old prophet. He is better understood as heralding the kingdom of God 'in the spirit and power of Elijah' (Luke 1.17).

John was undoubtedly a prophet in his own right – not at the end of the old order, but at the beginning of the new. He conducted his end-times prophetic ministry with authority, teaching people that judgement was at hand. He had a clear grasp of eschatology, always urging the people to live mindful of the reckoning that was to come. He solemnly reminded his listeners, 'Even now the axe is lying at the root of the trees; every tree therefore that does not bear good fruit is cut down and thrown into the fire . . . His winnowing-fork is in his hand, and he will clear his threshing floor' (3.10–12, NRSV). John wanted them to know that God's judgement requires obedience now, before it is too late.

John spoke truth and cared little about whether or not people liked him or his message. That seems difficult to grasp in our own culture, where a whole day might be spoiled if we lose a few followers on a Twitter thread. We are used to people flattering and applauding others because adulation matters to them. Not so for John. He was not seeking affirmation. We might even say he courted unpopularity, almost going out of his way to confront the hypocrisy of the religious establishment. Matthew ascribes to John (3.7–8) words that bluntly condemn insincerity and double standards; words that pre-empt those we later find in denunciations from Jesus. Inevitably, it brought John no favour from those in high places. People labelled a 'brood of vipers' are hardly going to feel endearment towards the speaker. Yet John continued to challenge hypocrisy, and his bid for integrity became total. The cost of his non-compromising stand is revealed in the chapters that follow. Not hesitating to expose the immorality of Herod, he faced the manipulation of Herodius, Herod's sister-in-law, and the moral weakness of Herod Antipas himself. The terrible story of Salome's dance and Herod's pathetic, reckless promise of any gift she wanted, up to half his kingdom, brought a result that the king had never intended. John died a martyr's death (14.3–12) rather than deny the truth. He was indeed a herald, preparing the way for Jesus, not simply in preaching repentance but also in living out his convictions.

Yet in many aspects John's ministry was very unlike that of Jesus. John expected the people to come to him, to confess and repent and be baptized. Jesus went to the people, to be among them and bring healing and help. John was an austere figure who had his own disciples but seemed to be always at a distance. Jesus spent many hours in close company teaching his disciples. John was mostly a recluse. Jesus was congenial to the point of being accused of fraternizing with sinners and being a wine-drinker and glutton (11.19). Not that John brimmed with unbridled self-confidence, however. He had his own doubts and insecurities, and once needed reassurance that Jesus was really the one who was to come. Jesus, however, faced the terror of Gethsemane with fear but without doubt.

John the Baptist shared the characteristics common to all prophets. He had powerful spiritual discernment, which came from God. He was aware of both his strengths and his limitations and was committed to pointing out what was wrong and calling those in power to account. But he was also ultimately impotent to right the wrong itself. That was out of his jurisdiction. Ronald Rolheiser sees that as significant for all of us.

> In essence, that's what we bring to any situation when we criticize something. We are able, often with brilliance and clarity, to show what's wrong. That contribution, like John the Baptist's, is not to be undervalued. The Gospels tell us that, next to Jesus, there isn't anyone more important than John the Baptist. But, like for John, criticism too is only a half-job, a half-prophecy: It can denounce a king by showing what's wrong, and it can wash the soul in sand, by blasting off layers of accumulated rust and dirt, but ultimately it can't empower us to correct anything. Something else is needed.[2]

That something else is the redemptive power of Jesus. Even when prophets draw others to repentance, they cannot of themselves give any absolution. When, as modern prophets, Christians are called to speak into what is wrong, or highlight injustice, we need, like John, to point to the one who can also forgive and heal.

Jesus gave his own accolade to John: 'among those born of women there has not risen anyone greater than John the Baptist' (11.11) – a statement he further endorsed by going to John to be baptized. John knew his significance lay in the person who came after him, whose sandals, he admitted, he was 'not worthy to carry' (3.11, NRSV). John, in another Gospel, is recorded as comparing himself to a best man who waits for the bridegroom and is overjoyed when he finally hears the bridegroom's voice. He is very happy to fade into the background while the focus increases on the groom. The famous pledge of humility, 'He must increase, but I must decrease' (John 3.30, NRSV) was made by John. Matthew also saw John in this light. Though John was the one to announce the coming of the kingdom and call people to repentance and faith, he knew that Jesus alone was able to take God's work through to fulfilment.

The role of John the Baptist was therefore key in Jesus' preparation for ministry. His was the voice of warning to the people, sounding the need for repentance and bringing them to baptism. And just as the people of his time met God through John's challenging message, Matthew invites us too to hear John's words of truth and integrity and let them sink in. For though he was neither the Messiah nor Elijah, he was someone whose message brings life and draws us closer to God.

The baptism of Jesus (Matthew 3)

I noted earlier that people came to John, whereas Jesus went to people. That is exactly what happened in Jesus' baptism. He went to John. He travelled from Galilee to the river Jordan to be baptized. The Jordan, of course, had many echoes of history, which Matthew would have known. The Israelites crossed the river Jordan on their way to the promised land (Joshua 3–4), Naaman dipped himself in the river Jordan to be healed from his leprosy (2 Kings 5.1–17). The waters of the Jordan signalled freedom and deliverance, pointing to the ongoing activity of God in the lives of people. It is not surprising that Jesus made his way to that river. Ian Paul points out: 'Matthew gives the impression that this is a de-termined decision by Jesus, crossing territories from Galilee through the Decapolis and Perea, to join John's eschatolog-ical renewal movement that is looking for the imminent coming of the kingdom of God.'[3]

It seems an appropriate explanation of why Jesus trav-elled that distance. Yet he could have identified with John's 'eschatological renewal movement' without being baptized. When John immediately recognized Jesus we can certain-ly understand his reluctance to baptize him. Although John himself might have needed a baptism of repentance, Jesus did not. What was more, John had already relativized his own 'water baptism' and signalled up that one would follow him with the 'baptism of the Holy Spirit and fire'. So why, then, did Jesus come to John to be baptized?

Curiously, in Matthew's account Jesus replies to John's misgivings in the plural: 'Let it be so now; it is proper for us to do this to fulfil all righteousness' (3.15). It is a statement of interdependence, where he draws John into fellowship with his own calling. Matthew makes it clear that John's role is important to Jesus: he is the baptizer sent by God in anticipation of Jesus' own ministry, and Jesus comes to re-ceive from John what John has to offer.

Throughout the Gospels we see Jesus pointing to the sig-nificance of the faith-offerings of other people. He repeat-edly shows he is ready to receive from them. Whether it is a drink of water from the Samaritan woman at the well (John 4), the relief of tired feet from the woman who rushes tearfully to kiss and anoint them (Luke 7.36–48) or the gift of loaves and fishes from a boy in the crowd (John 6.8–9), Jesus discloses his own vulnerability and accepts what other people have to offer him. And here, as Jesus comes in humility to baptism, we are quietly challenged about the human tendency to arrogance, self-promotion and entitlement.

Jesus' baptism is also about his identification with others, for many were coming to John to be baptized, prompted by the Holy Spirit to respond to God who promises salvation and new life. Matthew presents Jesus' baptism as both an affirmation of that new life and a statement of solidarity. Ian Paul writes:

> [F]or Matthew, Jesus' ministry of healing and deliverance is about his identification with them. We will read in Matt 8:17 that his ministry fulfils words from Is 53:5: 'He took up our infirmities and bore our diseases'. Later, we will read that he will 'offer his life as a ransom for many' (Matt 20:28) and will shed his blood for their forgiveness (Matt 26:28).
>
> Jesus cannot represent the people unless he identifies with them, and this identification begins with John's baptism as Jesus demonstrates his solidarity with this movement who are preparing for God's kingship over his people.[4]

If we had any doubt about the significance of Jesus' baptism, Matthew's description of what happens next would put our minds at rest. It is one of those rare moments when the heavens open and God is revealed. In 3.16 Matthew hints at an echo of Ezekiel's experience: 'while I was among the

33

exiles by the River Kebar, the heavens were opened and I saw visions of God' (Ezekiel 1.1). The image of Jesus coming out of the water, the voice of God the Father, and the Holy Spirit alighting on Jesus in the form of a dove together present a compelling Trinitarian vision of God's divinity. Matthew certainly leaves us in no doubt of the significance of this for Jesus' identity. The voice from heaven affirms it all. Jesus is the Son, the Beloved, with whom God is well pleased. The vision is sudden and powerful; one of those dramatic moments in the biblical narrative. Poetry conveys it, paintings celebrate it. It is not surprising that Giotto, Rubens, da Vinci, El Greco and so many more have found deep inspiration from the Gospel account of Jesus' baptism and made their own response in art.

Yet we also recognize that these moments are rare. Most of Matthew's Gospel is not like this. Matthew is content to show God working in gentler ways, quietly bringing to fulfilment in copious manifestations the yet-incomplete work of God indicated by the prophets in the Hebrew Scriptures. In reading this Gospel we can be glad that we have both the spectacular and the everyday, the dramatic and the peaceful. For it is in all these ways that we can encounter the love and power of God.

The temptations in the wilderness (Matthew 4)

In Matthew's account of Jesus' preparation in the wilderness we're reminded that although the wilderness was John's natural environment, it was not so for Jesus. Matthew tells us he was there only because of the leading of the Holy Spirit and for one simple purpose: to be tempted by the devil. In setting his scene so clearly, we might expect Matthew to describe Jesus as facing intense spiritual struggle, perhaps even going through a dark night of the soul, wrestling with doubts and fears, uncertain about continuing with the task ahead. But we get none of this. We have little dramatic interplay; certainly no hyperbole. You might even say that Matthew is the master of understatement. He tells us simply that after 40 days and nights of fasting, Jesus was hungry!

And yet we should not trivialize this account of the temptations. Whether Matthew spells it out for us or not, fasting traditionally foreshadowed a great spiritual struggle. Again, his readers would know that from the Hebrew Scriptures. Matthew did not need to tell them that both Moses and Elijah fasted for 40 days and nights and that the outcome for them was spectacular. Moses came down from his fast on Mount Sinai with a shining face and the tablets of stone on which were inscribed the Ten Commandments (Exodus 34.28–29). Elijah ended his fast at Mount Horeb, experiencing the power of wind, earthquake and fire before he finally encountered God in the still small voice (1 Kings 19.12). For Jesus too the period of fasting brought an exposure to spiritual struggles and attacks from the evil one. This is for many a deeply human experience. When any of us go through a spiritual ordeal, perhaps even during times of hardship or loss, we can be reassured that Jesus has been there too.

The three temptations were specific to Jesus. Even though some of us might face temptations that are similar, the ingredients will be very different. The first was to turn stones into bread and satisfy his hunger. Since this was well within his powers it seems odd at first for Matthew to present this as a temptation. Why not create food? It would be an efficient way of gaining nourishment, and Jesus would do this for others later in his ministry. Yet here, it would have been a misuse of power over the material world, exercising it simply for his own advantage to satisfy his own wants. It would have been going back on his fast, giving up on disciplined living when it became hard. The temptation was not just about food, but about self-preoccupation and self-interest.

The second temptation was to use a miracle to assert his identity. By throwing himself down from the pinnacle of the Temple to be upheld by angelic forces, he could let everyone see his importance and status. Uncertainties about his divine origin would have disappeared and he could have satisfied doubts from his detractors instantly. But the whole of Jesus' life to this point had been going in a different direction. Born in a cowshed, fleeing into Egypt to avoid Herod's baby cull, learning a carpenter's trade from his father, travelling with the crowds to worship in Jerusalem, what would all that have been about? This alternative speaks of ostentation, a spectacular display to gain prestige from others and show power in a terrifying way. It was refused.

The third temptation was simply one of idolatry. The temptation to gain political power, to have authority over all the kingdoms of the world presently in the grip of the evil one, was offered to Jesus on a plate. He did not need to face rejection and hardship; he did not need to go through suffering and the cross. The price was simply that Jesus in his earthly pilgrimage would worship the devil rather than the Father.

Although the temptations were unique to Jesus and had to be faced by him alone, they do speak into our lives in the world today. Take the first temptation. The underlying script is that we must enjoy the lifestyle to which we feel entitled, whatever the cost to anyone else. We are worth it. We do not need to live with basic resources when we have the means to enjoy ourselves. Consequently, though we live in a world where people suffer and go hungry, where our climate is overheating and the vulnerable are exploited, so many of those of us who can, live in affluent indifference. Consumerism has gripped so much of the world that we now see it as normal to lose the biodiversity of our planet, to allow the extinction of species, experience the spread of viral diseases and leave the poorest in the world to pick up the tab. Tragically, those with power to bring change can let concern about profits and short-term gain blinker the resolve to take the practical measures needed.

This temptation has echoes too in the way personal problems are approached. It's not unusual for people yearning for meaning to try to find material solutions to spiritual hunger. A holiday in the Bahamas might mask the restlessness of our hearts; a new kitchen might sort out a fractious family life; expensive things for our children might compensate for lack of deeper conversations. Except, of course, stuff doesn't work like this. Human beings cannot live by bread alone, but by every word that comes from the mouth of God. Jesus' answer wakens us to the deeper issues that need spiritual healing. And when we live his way, we might well find there is no incompatibility between living with basic resources and being deeply blessed by God.

We move to the second temptation. The script is about self-importance and identity. Wanting the adulation of the public might be a particular weakness of celebrities or sports stars, but vanity or pride is to be found in most of us. Narcissists are so self-obsessed that other people exist only as a foil to their self-interest. And the search for identity is one of the big searches of our age. Tragically, the fear of being nobody has driven some people to commit terrible acts of cruelty or self-vandalism to prove their importance.

Henri Nouwen sees self-importance and insecurity as often linked: 'When we have come to believe the voices that call us worthless and unlovable, then success, popularity and power are easily perceived as attractive solutions.'[5] But at a spiritual level they solve nothing. For Nouwen and Rolheiser a much better solution is to know our identity before God, and enjoy being blessed for who we are. Jesus knew who he was, so could respond authentically. There was no need for God to put him to the test:

In essence, what Jesus says when the devil challenges him to throw himself off the top of the temple to prove his specialness is this: 'I'll take the stairs down, just like everyone else!' Our blessedness is not predicated on having a VIP elevator, or on having any special privileges that set us apart from others. We are God's blessed ones, even when we find ourselves riding the city buses.[6]

In many ways, the third temptation is the hardest of all to defeat. Idolatry has become normalized in much of life. We don't recognize who or what we are worshipping because we are simply following a cultural norm. Whether it is money, power, sex, possessions, family, ideas or food, if something takes the place of God in our lives, then we are out of kilter with who we really are and what we were created for. Matthew makes a powerful point when he tells us the devil was able to show Jesus the kingdoms of the world and claim ownership of them. He could do this because he was worshipped there. That doesn't mean the people in those cultures were active Satan-worshippers who practised child sacrifice or cannibalism. They were just normal people going about their daily business. But their business was already structured by the institutions and values that society operated by, and those had been captured by forces in opposition to the goodness of God.

The tragedy about idolatry is that it seeps into our soul unawares. We do not always recognize when the switch has taken place. Idolatry can twist anything that is good and wholesome, even life-giving, into becoming the focus of our worship. C. S. Lewis expresses this so well in *The Four Loves*:

We may give our human loves the unconditional allegiance which we owe only to God. Then they become gods: then they become demons. Then they will destroy us, and also destroy themselves. For natural loves that are allowed to become gods do not remain loves. They are still called so but can become in fact complicated forms of hatred.[7]

The eighteenth-century Christian poet William Cowper knew this, as we can see in the hymn he wrote:

The dearest idol I have known,
Whate'er that idol be,
Help me tear it from thy throne,
And worship only thee.[8]

This is why Christian meditation is important. When we give ourselves time to reflect more deeply on our worship of God, we can discover those areas of idolatry in our lives that may have become hidden even from ourselves. The only safe response to the third temptation is the one that Jesus gave: 'Away from me, Satan! For it is written: "Worship the Lord your God, and serve him only"' (4.10).

We could summarize all these temptations of Jesus as being enticements to short cuts. Jesus came into the world to fulfil a mission that was costly and difficult. To see it through, Jesus knew he had to face hardship, rejection, injustice, persecution and death. Satan tempted him to achieve the outcome without the pain: to turn bread into stones; to assert his identity without being persecuted; to obtain authority over the kingdoms of the world from the devil. But Jesus refused, quoting the Hebrew Scriptures as his resource. Yet Matthew shows that enormous integrity was needed to fulfil those Scriptures; there was no place for cutting corners.

One final observation concerns the location of the temptations. Matthew reminds us that it was the desert, a wild and empty place, void of food and sustenance, offering little protection. That might have resonances for some of us. For people today, the desert can be experienced anywhere: in the workplace, in the middle of town or even at home. The emptiness and loneliness of the desert can fill our horizons and reach into our very souls. Yet, as Ronald Rolheiser believes, it can also lead to life:

The desert, as we know, is the place where, stripped of all that normally nourishes and supports us, we are exposed to chaos, raw fear, and demons of every kind. In the desert we are exposed, body and soul, made vulnerable to be overwhelmed by chaos and temptations of every kind. But, precisely because we are so stripped of everything we normally rely on, this is also a privileged moment for grace. Why? Because all the defence mechanisms, support systems, and distractions that we normally surround ourselves with . . . what we use to buoy us up, wards off both chaos and grace, demons and the divine alike. Conversely, when we are helpless, we are open. That is why the desert is both the place of chaos and the place of God's closeness.[9]

Matthew's narrative encourages us to believe this, for he lets us know that at the end of Jesus' temptations, the devil does depart and the angels come to minister to him. As we reflect on the temptations in our own lives and pray for God's strength and power to overcome them, may we also know the comfort of ministering angels.

Calling the disciples (Matthew 4, 10, 16)

The fourth aspect of Jesus' preparation for ministry seems in many ways to have been the easiest. Matthew describes the calling of the first disciples as almost a casual encounter. Two fishermen, Simon Peter and his brother Andrew, were casting a net when Jesus invited them to become fishers of people. Two more fishermen, James and John, were with Zebedee, their father, in a boat when they too were asked by Jesus to be his followers.

Matthew gives us no information about why they accepted this as the right thing to do. To us it might seem an extraordinary move to give up a livelihood to become students of an itinerant rabbi. Yet Matthew doesn't need to justify the response of the fishermen, because it was part of the process of discipleship deemed normal in the Jewish tradition. To be called by a learned rabbi to become an apprentice and a travelling companion was indeed a privilege; an invitation to model life on that of the rabbi and become like him. A disciple was someone who not only learned from his teacher but who absorbed his outlook, imitated his lifestyle and then taught others.

We see this in Jesus' commissioning of the disciples. Matthew relates how they themselves were sent out to the 'lost sheep of Israel', to preach and tell the people that the kingdom of heaven was at hand. He gave them authority to proclaim the good news, to heal the sick, cleanse the lepers, raise the dead and perform exorcisms (10.1–15). They had to show both shrewdness and innocence and seek out the people of peace. But as 'sheep among wolves' his key requirement was that they embraced vulnerability and remained dependent on him. In hostile terrain sheep do not survive long unless they are tended by the shepherd. Jesus warned his disciples that they would face opposition, even persecution. They were likely to be a long way out of their comfort zone, confronting interrogation and arrest. Yet they were not to be afraid, because the Holy Spirit would teach them how to respond. Whatever they were going through, they would be under the care of the God who knew everything about them: even the number of hairs on their heads!

Jesus made very high demands of those entering discipleship, probably far greater than most rabbis. In a later passage in the Gospel (16.24–26), Matthew records how he spelled out the cost:

> 'Whoever wants to be my disciple must deny themselves and take up their cross and follow me. For whoever wants to save their life will lose it, but whoever loses their life for me will find it. What good will it be for someone to gain the whole world, yet forfeit their soul? Or what can anyone give in exchange for their soul?'

Self-denial is writ large; the image of taking up their cross, with all its connotations of death and suffering, is a graphic one. It's a curious passage, for it also has a double focus. Jesus is saying that although the cost of following him is great, the cost of holding on to their own autonomy and will is even greater.

We have few domestic details of the way Jesus and his disciples lived. In Matthew's story no mention is made of how the disciples would now earn their living, but his early readers would probably already have known that hospitality and support would be provided as Jesus and his followers journeyed from town to town and blessed the people. We know from the Gospel of Luke that a number of women followers supported Jesus and the disciples from their own means (Luke 8). Jesus had begun preaching and by the time he called the first four fishermen, his lifestyle would have been well established. From then onwards, they shared it together.

Matthew gives us a full list of the disciples later in his Gospel, but we have scant knowledge of their backgrounds. Few, if any, had noble standing. Eli seemed relatively wealthy and was recorded as providing hospitality himself. Matthew had been a tax collector, an occupation despised by Jews reluctant to pay taxes to Roman occupiers. Simon, by contrast, was a Zealot, part of a political group in opposition to the Roman government, so conversations about past experiences of life must have been interesting! Most of the others had been fishermen.

The disciples were a key group both in the life of Jesus and the early Church. They travelled with him, were taught by him and became observers of his healings and miracles. When he asked his disciples who they believed he was, Peter replied without hesitation that he was the Messiah, Son of the living God (16.13–20). The disciples were eyewitnesses to the feeding of vast crowds, to Gentiles coming in faith to Jesus to ask for healing for other people they cared for, to individuals receiving forgiveness from God. They watched and listened to the opposition of religious authorities. They were constantly warned by Jesus about the cost of following him, and they also let him down. Matthew describes the loneliness of Gethsemane as Jesus prayed in agony while his disciples failed to stay awake. Then at his hour of greatest need, one disciple betrayed him, one denied him, and many of them fled rather than face persecution from the authorities. But they also witnessed the supremacy and sovereignty of God in the resurrection of Jesus. And it was these followers who would experience the empowering of the Holy Spirit, lay the foundation of the Church and go on to become martyrs for their faith.

The time of preparation had been well spent. Jesus was ready to take up his ministry to the people around him. And Matthew's Gospel begins its focus on Jesus' teaching of the kingdom, and the signs and wonders that went with his message. As crowds came to receive his words and open their own lives to the love of God, we too can open our hearts to absorb the truth of the kingdom of heaven.

3

Meeting God in the teaching of the kingdom

When Matthew tells us John the Baptist said that 'the kingdom of heaven' had come near, it was the first of some 30 references Matthew would make in his Gospel. He next mentions the kingdom of heaven in relation to Jesus going through Galilee, teaching in synagogues and 'proclaiming the good news of the kingdom' (4.23). A few chapters later Matthew tells us again: 'Jesus went throughout all the towns and villages, teaching in their synagogues, proclaiming the good news of the kingdom and healing every disease and every illness' (9.35). In between these two summaries Matthew shows us how this kingdom takes shape in Jesus' teaching, preaching and powerful ministry of love. Step by step we find that it is so radically different from the ways of the world or the cultural values practised across the globe. It is a kingdom that God inhabits as King, and whose citizenship we must seek if we are to meet and know God.

Our first stage on the journey is the Sermon on the Mount. By now, crowds already follow Jesus, not only from Galilee, the area where most of his ministry takes place, but also from Decapolis, Jerusalem, Judea and other places beyond the Jordan. Something about this man's teaching and authority draws them to hear more. With the masses pressing in, Jesus goes up a hill with his disciples, and begins to teach.

The Sermon on the Mount
(Matthew 5 – 7)

The Sermon on the Mount may have been delivered by Jesus in a single session, or Matthew may have put together a series of his sermons so we can absorb the depth of his teaching in one reading. It doesn't matter which of these we opt for. What is more important is the content and direction of what is taught. The sermon is a definitive statement of Jesus' teaching, and its focus is the kingdom of heaven. We quickly realize that this is not an otherworldly, remote, spiritualized concept. It is earthy, demanding and radical, but altogether different from the way most of us see the world and live our lives. Even hearing the sermon read in church might not challenge us but inoculate us against its power. Sometimes we've had 'a low dose of the Sermon on the Mount for so long that we're immune to the full-strength version'. But the sermon is absolutely central to Jesus' teaching. I remember John Stott insisting that the Sermon on the Mount was a statement of 'Christian counterculture' and 'the nearest thing to a manifesto that [Jesus] ever uttered, for it is his own description of what he wanted his followers to be and to do'.[1]

The Sermon on the Mount was delivered by Jesus predominantly to his disciples. Yet it seems evident that others heard him too, because at the end of the sermon Matthew records that 'the crowds were amazed at his teaching, because he taught as one who had authority and not as their teachers of the law' (7.28–29). Whatever the size of the audience who heard it first hand, Jesus' sermon brings the reality of God into everyday life for ordinary people wherever they are. It is no exaggeration to say that his teaching on the kingdom is the foundry where our values must be shaped and our spiritual identities forged.

Jesus begins his hilltop sermon with the Beatitudes. The word 'beatitude' means 'to be blessed, to enjoy abundance'. He gives us statements describing those who are blessed. The Beatitudes are not a list of commands and prohibitions. They are not like the Ten Commandments. Many dos and don'ts come later in the sermon, but not here. First, Matthew shows us the times and conditions in which people can be blessed, or happy. Effectively, Jesus is addressing questions that human beings have asked since the beginning of history. How can we be happy? What sort of state is happiness? 'Well, as long as they're happy' is a refrain voiced by many anxious parents. Whatever it is, it seems to describe a basic longing people have to be content, 'at home' with themselves and untroubled. So Jesus says, 'You want to be happy? Well, listen carefully. Here's how . . .' And he goes on to show us what confers real blessings on our lives and what kind of 'happy people' we can become.

The eight Beatitudes all begin 'Blessed are . . .'. The first and the eighth refer to the kingdom of heaven present now, and those in between spell out what is promised in the future for people in certain states of life. We soon realize that in each of them Jesus completely undermines normal conceptions of what happiness is. He challenges his own culture, and ours, by taking those deemed to be at the bottom of the happiness pile and declaring the true state to be different. What really makes people happy turns out to be not what we think; we're not made happy through wealth, status or power. Happiness isn't conferred by opulent living, accumulation or being more successful than others. By contrast, yearning after these things brings insatiability rather than completeness and can take its toll on people's lives. One of the world's richest billionaires was once asked how much money he needed to be truly happy. His answer? 'Just a little bit more.'

In eight short phrases, then, Jesus reverses the perceptions and standards of the world. It's the meek who inherit the earth, not the ambitious, the driven or the self-seeking. It's those who hunger and thirst after right living who receive fullness, not those with lavish expense accounts and a full wine cellar. It's the poor in spirit who experience the joy of the kingdom, for they can see through the superficiality and glibness of this world and happily embrace what others might see as poverty. Jesus breaks every expectation of what it means to be truly happy or enjoy abundant life. Those who are happy trust God despite deprivation or hardship. When he uses the phrases 'Blessed are the merciful, for they will be shown mercy', 'Blessed are the pure in heart, for they will see God', 'Blessed are the peacemakers, for they will be called children of God', he is identifying these people as already living with the values of God's kingdom. And even those who are suffering experience blessing, whether they're mourning loss, undergoing persecution or facing injustice, for they are standing firm for God in a broken world. The kingdom of heaven is both here now and in the world to come. We live in it and we inherit it; we know it today and will absorb the blessings it brings in the future.

The Beatitudes are normally taken personally because they *are* personal. They are an echo of what is written by the prophets and in the psalms for people who are humble, merciful and peaceful in their relationships. Jesus is preaching from the core of the Hebrew Scriptures – not offering legalistic prerequisites, but describing the heart that will turn to God to be made content and fulfilled. Being blessed is about living in a state of grace. It is about our identity, who we are, not just what we do. So we are right to take them personally. We can seek to live transformed lives to God's glory because we know we are blessed.

But the Beatitudes are also world-changing structural principles. The poor in spirit are those who do not want to conquer and dominate. They choose peace rather than war; they refuse to double the heartache of those who already mourn. They are people living God's way. Similarly, the merciful are those who do not want to seek vengeance or annihilate dissidents. They are forgiving reconcilers. In contrast to the tyrants of his age and all ages, Jesus is setting up the parameters of the whole system of God's gentle world government. But how little we know of it in the geopolitics of our age.

The Beatitudes are not triumphalist but hard work. They do not offer us trouble-free lives. Being blessed children of God does not inoculate us against those who would cause harm and destroy, whether we are world leaders or children in the playground. But it does teach us to resist and pray for God's word to break through. It stamps our passport as citizens of the kingdom of heaven.

Having delivered his Beatitudes, Jesus then shows how kingdom values can affect the public world. His famous metaphor of being salt and light was a highly relevant image for his day. Salt brings out flavours, seasoning bland ingredients, and was crucial in those days for food preservation. In a warm climate with no refrigeration, meat without salt quickly went bad and became toxic rather than life-giving. But salt needs to be salty. Living in the kingdom requires disciples who make the earth a more palatable place by retaining their distinctiveness. Light too was essential, for finding the way and making things visible when darkness fell. Like salt, light had to be used. Lamps were to be placed where they were most effective, not hidden nor covered over. They had to be beacons in a dark world, revealing all that was good and exposing evil. Christians living as salt and light are essential in a world where rot can quickly set in and people live in darkness. In personal and public life we are called to display the kingdom of heaven, for this is where God has placed us.

The Sermon on the Mount now turns to Jesus' link with the Hebrew Scriptures and his fulfilment of the Law and Prophets. In the light of the kingdom, the Law now takes on a much bigger magnitude than anything presented by the scribes or Pharisees (5.21–48). Jesus' repeated refrain, 'You have heard that it was said . . . but I tell you . . .', pits superficial interpretations of moral behaviour against true right living. Jesus is not talking about any nominal, nittygritty rule-keeping, but redefining what it really means to fulfil the Law's demands; it emanates from the heart, not mere behaviour. Harbouring evil thoughts in your heart is the same as doing the acts. Nursing anger is akin to murder, lusting is akin to adultery, entertaining temptation is opening ourselves to sin. The result is an intensification of the Law, where we begin to see how murder, adultery, temptation or retaliation reach deeply into our lives. In his six commands, Jesus illustrates where the righteousness of Christ-followers has to exceed that of the religious rule-enforcers. They must replace lust with purity, infidelity with faithfulness, dishonesty with honesty, revenge with reconciliation. In the justice of the kingdom, mere recompense – 'an eye for an eye and a tooth for a tooth' – is no longer enough. We are to love our enemies.

It is never going to be easy to turn the other cheek, to refuse to return evil for evil, to let go of resentment and to love those who hate us. It was not the way the world operated when Jesus was on earth, nor has it been any time since. Those who lived under Roman occupation knew a great deal about injustice. Those who were forced by their taskmasters to endure long hours of work for little pay knew a great deal about economic exploitation. Similar oppressive regimes exist in our world today. Yet in urging the people towards peaceful relationships with others, Jesus is not condoning injustice. He is asking his listeners not to join the evil in the world but to follow a different way.

This comes out in the rest of the Sermon on the Mount. The 'do nots' that Jesus lists are in sharp contrast to the accepted ways of operating. He warns against self-promotion and affectation. We are not to give, to pray or to fast in order to impress other people. We are to do these things because they are part of kingdom living, where lives are open before God. We are not to be fixated on stuff, because possessions will take over our lives and hold us in bondage. We are not to have divided loyalties or crave wealth, because we will be drawn into idolatry and away from serving God, who cares for us. We are not to be anxious about tomorrow, but live one day at a time, trusting God who knows our needs. We are not to be self-righteous, judging other people while ignoring our own sin, but must consciously address our own faults. And we are not to fool ourselves so that we end up deluded, believing our own propaganda. Instead, our lives should always be open to God's spotlight and scrutiny.

At the centre of Jesus' message is simplicity and trust. We are to ask, search and knock, and have confidence that God understands what is right for us. In the complexity of life, the simple, transparent ways of living that Jesus points to free us from all kinds of bondage and taking the wrong path. He urges us to keep our eyes spiritually sound and develop clarity of vision. He commends simplicity of worship, as epitomized in the Lord's Prayer (6.7–14). He points to the generosity of God, reminding us that if we who are evil know how to give good things to our children, how much more our heavenly Father will give to those who ask (7.9–11)! He warns us to have discernment and recognize wolves in sheep's clothing – religious or political charlatans – who lead so many astray. And he reminds us to build on strong foundations, because consequences inevitably follow from the choices and decisions we make. Jesus closes his sermon with the famous parable of the wise and foolish men and the buildings they try to erect. We come away from his sermon knowing that if we hear and act on the words he has imparted to us, we will learn wisdom and begin to be effective in the kingdom of heaven.

Jesus preached the sermon a long time ago, but it is as important for our postmodern condition as it was for the legalism of the Pharisees. Yet we need to realize that it speaks now into a culture with different frames of reference. When Jesus told his hearers, 'You have heard that it was said . . .' they knew he was referring to the Law. In the secular cultures predominating in the West, it is not the Law that is our reference point but the demands of the self. The self's right to choose, even to 'self-identify', is sacrosanct. Today, 'You have heard that it was said' may refer to a 'plethora of voices, a myriad of opinions, ideals, and ideologies', as Ronald Rolheiser notes, for the secular age bombards us with options. He continues:

> Our predisposition is a moral duty to self . . . that late modern inflated entity that stands in place of the law and over and against God. In theory much is said about human rights and tolerance, but there is no moral foundation for saying it is wrong to hate my brother. The secular age replaces the beauty, purity, and fidelity of sex and the covenant of marriage with the notion of consensual sex. There is no higher purpose or meaning other than the satisfaction of the modern self's longings and desires.[2]

Life as citizens of the kingdom today brings different challenges. If legalism was a powerful religious enemy to take on then, institutionalized self-centredness is no less so today. Matthew's Gospel implies that we are to combat this in the same manner as the disciples. We are to listen, absorb, pray and act on the words of Jesus. The call to deny ourselves, take up our cross and follow Jesus (16.24–26) is a call to us as well as to them. For us, being countercultural may mean stripping ourselves of the vestiges of self-absorption and egotism and all sense of entitlement.

The Sermon on the Mount describes a kingdom of heaven that exists alongside all the kingdoms of this world. In every era it gives rise to what Lesslie Newbigin has described as 'a new plausibility structure, a radically different vision of things from those that shape all human cultures apart from the Gospel'.[3] It is a way of thinking, feeling, acting and living that embraces a view of reality profoundly different from that found in the world we live in. And today the challenge it offers us is every bit as important as it was to the first-century hearers on the hillside.

Signs and wonders in the kingdom

Matthew shows us other signs of the kingdom of heaven, for the Jesus who preaches and teaches the kingdom in the Sermon on the Mount is the same Jesus who performs miracles. Just as we met God in the kingdom Beatitudes, we meet God in the kingdom miracles. They seem to begin immediately in Matthew's account (8.1–17). Jesus is hardly down from the hilltop before a man with a leprous skin disease rushes to kneel before him. In faith, he affirms that if Jesus is willing, he can heal him. Jesus is willing and the man is healed. Then when Jesus arrives in Capernaum, a Roman centurion pleads with him to heal his servant. Marvelling at the faith of someone outside the Jewish community, Jesus does as he asks and the servant is restored. Jesus arrives at the house of Peter to find Peter's mother-in-law sick with fever. Jesus touches her hand and the fever goes. Later that evening, many people with a great variety of ailments come to Jesus, and through the outflow of miracles people are made better. As the stories continue, Matthew describes the release of a man possessed, the healing of someone who has long been paralysed, the restoring of sight to two people who are blind, the enabling of someone to speak, the curing of a woman's menstrual problems and the raising of a girl who has died (9.18–26).

By now we can see Jesus' authority over the medical and physical factors that affect the human body. But Matthew goes on to show us more. The authority of Jesus is over every part of creation. At the end of the day, now in a boat with his disciples, the little vessel is subjected to a fierce storm. As the lashing waves are about to overcome them, Jesus lies peacefully asleep. The terrified disciples wake him, fearful that they are about to drown, but Jesus' response is to rebuke their lack of faith and tell the wind and waves to calm down. We might well have asked the same question as the disciples: 'What kind of man is this? Even the winds and the waves obey him!' (8.23–27). In another dramatic miracle he takes a boy's gift of a few small loaves and fish and feeds the hungry crowd of people who have been listening to him all day; they number 5,000. A short time later he repeats the miracle and feeds 4,000 (15.32–39). Probably the most whimsical miracle is when he resolves a question of whether or not he should pay the temple tax by telling Peter to catch a fish and take the coin from its mouth to give to the tax collectors as their payment (17.24–27).

It is not long, however, before some of the miracles Jesus performs become controversial. The healing of two men possessed by evil spirits involves releasing the men from their spiritual bondage but transferring the problem into a herd of pigs. This might not have caused much consternation to Matthew's Jewish readers, for whom pigs were unclean animals and creatures to avoid, but the pigs' owners would not have been impressed when the pigs ran headlong down a hill to be drowned in the water (8.28–33). Other miracles challenge the Jewish authorities, especially those who see themselves as mediating the Law to the people. The healing of a man's withered hand on the Sabbath proves a huge bone of contention (12.9–14). The tragedy of this story is that the religious leaders are so caught up in legalism, they miss both the amazing miracle and the whole point of Sabbath worship of God.

The reason why the miracles are important is not simply because they demonstrated to the crowds that Jesus had power to heal. Matthew is clear about this. If they had been, why would Jesus have shunned the publicity and instructed those healed of leprosy or blindness to tell no one that he had healed them? And when the Pharisees came to him asking for a miracle, why would he have refused to give them their 'sign from heaven'? Matthew lets us know that Jesus was not producing signs and wonders to prove who he was. He had nothing to prove. Nor did he want people to start following him because he performed public spectacles. Jesus did not want his messiahship to be misunderstood. The people were expecting a messiah who demonstrated power, and who could whip up the crowds into following him.

But to where? To riots? Insurgence? To the overthrow of Israel's enemies by military might? Many had not yet understood the prophecy that the Messiah would be someone of compassion and gentleness who would not break the bruised reed or quench a smouldering flax. God's Anointed One would bind up the broken-hearted and set the captive free – quietly, unobtrusively reaching out to the vulnerable and bringing God's forgiveness to those who repented. He would even proclaim justice to the Gentiles. They had not yet understood what the Scriptures taught about the kingdom of heaven and about the King who would reign.

The real point about the miracles is not that they were miraculous, but that they were integral to who Jesus was. Matthew is showing us that the Jesus of the Sermon on the Mount is the same Jesus who healed the woman's bleeding, restored sight to those who could not see and stilled the storm. The miracles were integrated into his teaching, his relationships, his prayer life, prophecies in the Hebrew Scriptures and his call to repentance and faith. Everything Jesus did shows us more of the kingdom of heaven, and those who were healed, released, restored and renewed went through life-changing experiences that opened them up to a deeper relationship with God.

The miracles therefore have to be seen from the perspective of Jesus' teaching of the kingdom and his love. They were bound up with faith, as we see in the trust of the man with leprosy, the Roman centurion and the Canaanite woman. They were part of forgiveness, as was evident in the restoration of the paralysed man. They were linked with the fulfilment of prophecy, as Matthew mentioned in his story of healings and exorcisms in Capernaum. In none of these healings was Jesus performing miracles to make a point, and they were all in the context of something greater than the healing alone. At the heart of the miraculous was the outworking in the kingdom of God's power and authority, shown through the love of Jesus.

Something else is interesting about the miracles: their own prophetic nature. We could say that Jesus was also showing us what is possible in the creation itself about restoration and wholeness. It is a glimpse of the future, when miracles of healing will be everyday affairs. The people who came to Jesus were bringing their problems to God, and God was responding by saying: 'Look, I have made a world where people can be fed, leprosy can be cured, cataracts can be removed, sight restored, limbs put together again. You will see cleft lips remoulded, menstrual disorders treated, illnesses eradicated and PTSD addressed. Do not give up hope. Work for restoration.' Jesus brought this about through his miracles, but was affirming too that in the wonderful way the world is created, we harness God's power today each time we bringing healing to someone's body.

Parables of the kingdom

Jesus' teaching about the kingdom of heaven is also given in parables. Matthew highlights eight parables of the kingdom in chapter 13 that describe both the power of God's word to bear kingdom fruit and the need for those who hear it to be vigilant. As Jesus tells the crowds more and more about the demands of the kingdom of heaven, the division between those who reject his teaching and those who receive it becomes increasingly marked. These parables signal that those who accept God's word of life and those who reject it live together, but eventually 'a tree is recognized by its fruit' (12.33–37).

In the parable of the sower, the main focus is on the seed and the soil. The four different kinds of soil receive the same seed, but only one kind of soil produces the environment for growth and flourishing. Seed sown on pathways, rocky soil and areas choked by weeds stand little chance of putting down roots. In a short time, it is as if no seed was ever sown there. It is a clear picture of Christian outreach. When we deliver God's word, it is not difficult to recognize the strength of distracting factors in human life – unreceptiveness, shallowness, cares of the world and the lure of wealth. They are not dramatic in themselves, but all of them pull people away from the calling of the kingdom.

The next six parables all begin 'The kingdom of heaven is like . . .' and Jesus paints pictures of weeds among wheat, yeast leavening bread, the growth of a tiny mustard seed, treasure hidden in a field, a pearl of great price, and a net full of good and bad fish. The images powerfully convey the side-by-side living but different destinies of those serving the kingdom and those whose hearts are elsewhere. They also convey the cost of choosing the kingdom. It requires entering the 'narrow gate', walking the hard way, paying the price of discipleship and becoming a servant of others. Like the man finding field treasure and the merchant's priceless pearl, we have to give up everything else in order to possess it (13.44 –45).

However, for people involved in kingdom work there is huge reassurance in these parables. Three of them signal how effective the work can be. The parables of the sower, the yeast and the mustard seed are especially encouraging for those who find the going hard and feel they have little to show for it. Even though so much of the soil has been unproductive, and the wait is long, the sower eventually sees a great harvest, yielding thirty- to a hundredfold of grain. The woman baking bread takes a tiny amount of yeast and mixes it with three measures (about 40 litres) of meal, and produces enough bread for around a hundred people. The mustard seed is minute, yet eventually grows into a massive bush with branches reaching out to offer shelter. The key ingredients, seed or yeast, are effectively hidden and we do not always know what is happening, but something surely is. Kingdom work has its seasons, and the work we do through the Holy Spirit in one season bears fruit in another. The growth of the kingdom, vividly pictured in these parables, remains primarily an action of God, Lord of heaven and earth (11.25), who works with us and through us.

But there is encouragement at another level too. These parables also tell us that kingdom work blesses not only those who undertake it but all who come into contact with it. The yeast quietly leavens the dough. Our witness to the kingdom reaches out into our neighbourhoods, colleges and workplaces, and spreads truth and love into the lives of others. The mustard seed produces a bush so huge that even the birds of the air come and nest there. It's a picture of outreach, grace and hospitality spreading from the kingdom and God's people to bless those in need, whether that need is for refuge, homes, food or justice.

It is wonderful to know that Christians have been fulfilling the teaching in these parables. So many organizations, caring churches and group initiatives have taken the kingdom into the community and made a difference. Food banks, advisory centres, care for the elderly, soup kitchens, debt workshops have all sprung up to share the hospitality of the kingdom of heaven. Sometimes the call is unexpected and costly.

My friend Ed Walker suddenly saw with utmost clarity the need for Christian action for the homeless and could not rest until he had responded to this vision. He and his wife Rachel stepped out in faith, mortgaged their home and threw themselves tirelessly into the task of providing homes, support, friendship and love for people who were homeless and marginalized. Over the years their initiative, Hope into Action, partnered with churches and individuals to make homes and care available to forgotten people in the shadows. A true kingdom venture, it was recognized beyond the Church, with public service awards from *The Guardian* and the Centre for Social Justice.[4]

Characteristics of kingdom relationships

Letting go of worry

Worry and anxiety are common human characteristics, and in his teaching on the kingdom Jesus acknowledges that. He lists our trivial worries – what we should wear, or eat or drink – and shows how pointless they are. But in the kingdom of heaven we are told to let go of even deeper anxieties. Jesus makes two key points. Worry achieves nothing, and worry crowds out trust. We cannot add a single hour to our life through worry, and God knows what we need and will provide it.

Letting go of worry is not the same as being indifferent. If we are indifferent to the things that others worry about it does not automatically mean that we are trusting God to teach us what matters. It may be, rather, that we are people who lack empathy or are oblivious to suffering or hardship. Jesus understands well that there are many reasons for people's anxiety. There may be trouble ahead; tomorrow will have its problems. But if we drag those problems into today, we are heading for a day of trouble and anxiety. So the kingdom vision helps us not to anticipate tomorrow's problems. We live prepared for what we have to face, but live without fear, trusting in God's love and compassion one day at a time.

Being childlike

The kingdom of heaven reverses so many of our values and assumptions. One of them is about children. They are to be our role models. Rather than see great leaders, entrepreneurs or intellectuals as our prototypes, Jesus tells us: 'unless you change and become like little children, you will never enter the kingdom of heaven' (18.3). This seems a strange idea, since maturity, especially Christian maturity, is prized elsewhere in the Scriptures. Even the disciples had not grasped this, because they scolded the mothers who brought children for Jesus to bless. Jesus' rebuke to his disciples, and his insistence that the children be encouraged, reinforced his earlier statement: 'for the kingdom of heaven belongs to such as these' (19.14). It seems that a childlike attitude is a universal requirement for entry to the kingdom. Jesus even thanked his Father that things hidden from the wise had been revealed to small children (11.25). What is it, then, about children that we need to note and emulate?

We can find a whole theology of childhood in the New Testament. A child's trust, vulnerability, openness, spontaneity and readiness to believe (21.16) are all kingdom assets. So is their humility. For people who possess humility know they have something to learn. They don't look down on others, assume they are right or push themselves forward. People with humility don't take priority over others or make sure their wants are satisfied first. These assets of childhood are for us to learn from and appropriate, and Jesus implicitly commends them.

Jesus' references to children have, of course, other implications for us today. He speaks of the faith of 'little ones' and tells us their angels will hold us accountable to God for the way they are treated. He also warns against those who would violate or harm children, and his words are extraordinarily forceful (18.6–7). It would be better for them to have a heavy millstone round their neck and be drowned in the sea. Rarely does Jesus speak with such vehemence. But the kingdom of heaven honours children and requires us to see childhood as a vital and authentic period of life.

The implications of this go beyond safeguarding or preventing bullying. They include not exposing children to adult behaviour patterns, not targeting them through advertising, not requiring them to act beyond their years and not passing on to them our distorted values. They mean giving children boundaries and parenting them in a way that reflects the loving parenthood of God. These sharp, simple statements from Jesus challenge the whole contemporary culture in which we care for children and bring them to adulthood.

Showing forgiveness

The kingdom of heaven has implications for all our relationships, including those that break down, especially within a church. Jesus is well aware that his followers may not always agree with one another and envisions a situation where two Christians are at loggerheads (18.15–22). How should it be dealt with? Disagreement is understandable, especially when we remember that the body of Christ is made up of such diverse people – in background, age, gender, temperament and ability. But where there is offence it must be dealt with. Jesus outlines clear steps.

The person wronged should tell the offender. If that produces understanding and reconciliation, then fellowship is restored. If not, then one or two others need to be involved pastorally, and if that doesn't work, others in the church should hear of the issue. It's important, however, to note that Jesus' role for the church here is pastoral. The church is there to listen and help, not to adjudicate and discipline. If the offence is real but the offender still refuses to recognize it and repent, then the offended may break off the relationship with that person, because there can be no reconciliation. This is not, as some have interpreted, the church enacting excommunication. It is simply interpersonal. Jesus is speaking only to the wronged individual, telling the person to walk away. For who knows what the effect might be? Time out of that relationship may give the other space to think and seek a better outcome.

For the disciple Peter this raises the question of forgiveness. Assuming wrong is acknowledged, are we still expected to go on forgiving someone who continues to do wrong things? Seven times even? Jesus' famous answer, 'not seven times, but seventy-seven times', indicates that there is no limit to our requirement to forgive. He drives the point home in yet another parable of the kingdom of heaven. The kingdom of heaven is like a lord who forgives a debt. The astronomical debt a servant owes to his lord is cancelled. But the servant shows no mercy towards the one who owes him a very small amount and treats him cruelly. The other servant sees the injustice of this, and the lord reacts, withdrawing his original generous provision. Dick France comments on what the parable teaches us about grace and forgiveness: '[A]ny limitation on the forgiveness he shows his brother is unthinkable. The fact that the second servant's debt is one six-hundred thousandth of the first emphasises the ludicrous impropriety of the forgiven sinner standing on his own rights.'[5]

Forgiveness and reconciliation remains a hugely challenging area for human beings. The breakdown of relationships causes anger, bitterness and wars, and can pass down through the generations. In the kingdom of heaven we are urged to reach out to those who offend us, to confess our own faults and seek forgiveness. And Jesus affirms that those who are forgiven are called to forgive others. Restoration is a wonderful alternative to acrimony and resentment.

The kingdom and the King

At the very heart of the kingdom of heaven is the King who rules in gentleness and mercy, in faithfulness and compassion. It is a kingdom of peace where the wolf will live with the lamb, the leopard lie down with the goat, and a child shall lead them (Isaiah 11.6). It is a kingdom where swords will be beaten into ploughshares and spears into pruning hooks. 'Nation will not take up sword against nation, nor will they train for war any more' (Isaiah 2.4). Spurgeon rejoices in its radical nature: 'Strange kingdom, in which there is the palm without the sword, the victory without the battle. No blood, no tears, no devastation, no burned cities, no mangled bodies! King of peace, King of peace, this is thy dominion!'[6]

In Matthew's kingdom concept we also find the closeness and warmth of God, for the kingdom of heaven is also the kingdom of the Father. Royal metaphors and family metaphors are closely associated. We see this especially in Jesus' explanation of the parable of the weeds, where 'the righteous will shine like the sun in the kingdom of their Father' (13.43). When Peter makes his confession of Jesus as the Messiah, he is told that this was revealed to him by the Father in heaven. When we do our good works before people, it is our 'Father in heaven' who is glorified (5.16). When we love our enemies, we are 'children of [our] Father in heaven' (5.45). We are to be perfect as our 'heavenly Father is perfect' (5.48). Even the Lord's Prayer begins 'Our Father in heaven' and continues 'your kingdom come'. The understanding of 'heaven' in Matthew was never a place above the sky, as critics often assume. It is the realm of God's existence, the whole cosmos:

> God is the Creator, the horizon of his kingdom is cosmic in character. The coming of the kingdom is not merely directed towards saving souls for heaven. In the Sermon on the Mount the righteousness required of the citizens of God's kingdom covers the totality of human existence. And in the concluding verses of Matthew, Jesus speaks as the mighty King whose authority covers the entire universe, and whose commission encompasses 'all nations' (Mt 28:19–20).[7]

We can see, then, that Matthew's understanding of the kingdom of heaven is wider than what we understand as the Church. As Herman Ridderbos points out in his magisterial work, the Church (*ekklesia*) is the people who have been 'gathered together by the preaching of the Gospel and will inherit the redemption of the kingdom now and in the great future'. The Church is the instrument of the kingdom, as it preaches Jesus the Messiah and lives as his body on earth. But the kingdom is universal in scope. It 'represents the all-embracing perspective, it denotes the consummation of all history, brings both grace and judgment, has cosmic dimensions, fills time and eternity'.[8]

Jesus' teaching of the kingdom of heaven in Matthew's Gospel is radical, powerful and demanding. It is nothing less than the transformation of the whole of our lives, so we can live them in the service of the King, who also serves. We are called to do this in a fallen world, the values, ambitions and goals of which are so different from the ones Jesus sets before us. Yet it is the calling of every Christian, and resources are given to us to fulfil it. We are not alone. We are encompassed around with the grace of God and the power of the Holy Spirit.

4

Meeting God on the journey to Jerusalem

Jesus has been ministering in Galilee, but Matthew now changes the panorama for us. He is ready to set out for Jerusalem.

Jerusalem, set on a hill 900 metres above sea level, was the centre of Jewish life and religion. Pilgrims across the land went to the City of David three or four times a year. We know from the Gospel of John that Jesus was among them, and probably made several individual journeys to Jerusalem during his ministry. As an observant Jewish man, it would have been normal to join worshippers at major festivals. We read that he healed at the pool of Bethesda on the Sabbath (John 5.1–18) and taught in the Temple during the Festival of Booths (John 7.10–24). He was also threatened with stoning during the Festival of the Dedication (John 10.31–38). The other three New Testament Gospels do not record these separate visits to Jerusalem, although Luke writes of Jesus being presented as a baby at the Temple, and then as a twelve-year-old being inadvertently left behind in Jerusalem after the Passover. In Matthew's Gospel, the ordering of the events of Jesus' life is topical or thematic rather than purely chronological, so just as he gives us his major Sermon on

the Mount, Matthew also focuses on one single major cataclysmic journey to Jerusalem. All four Gospels describe
Jesus' triumphal entry into the city with the colt and the
crowds and the cries of 'Hosanna!'

Matthew's account of the journey begins as Jesus and
his disciples leave Galilee to travel through Judea beyond
the Jordan (19.1). Those in the crowds who follow him are
taught and healed as before, but despite the ministry en
route, we are left in no doubt that their destination hangs
somewhat ominously over the travelling group. The journey
is very intentional; Jesus knows where he is going and why.
His decision to go there is a deliberate choice to face opposition. He knows he has enemies ahead of him.

Matthew is hardly an impartial bystander in the di-
vergence between the religious authorities and Jesus. It is
very clear he is writing his account as one who has been
convinced by Jesus and wants to tell his hearers about the
difference in their positions. Matthew lets us know that
these leaders showed no thankfulness to God that people
were being healed in his name and brought to a new life of
faith and praise. Nor did they benefit from having a teacher
in their midst with such wisdom and discernment. Instead,
their resentment grew with every encounter. We realize
from Matthew's account that the antagonism of the religious establishment towards Jesus was not only related to
different interpretations of the Law. They also found Jesus'
associations distasteful. Jesus says as much when he comments about their judgements: 'John came neither eating
nor drinking, and they say, "He has a demon." The Son of
Man came eating and drinking, and they say, "Here is a

glutton and a drunkard, a friend of tax collectors and sin-ners." But wisdom is proved right by her deeds' (11.18–19). To be a powerful rabbinical teacher and yet associate with the 'immoral' and marginalized was certainly beyond the pale. Even deeper, however, was his exposure of their own superficial spirituality and hypocrisy, and his resistance to-wards their legalism.

This latter issue had already had an airing. Matthew tells how, while he was still in Galilee, the scribes and Pharisees had come as a delegation from Jerusalem to investigate Jesus. The interview with him started badly when they asked why his disciples were not obeying the ablutions laws and following the extensive handwash-ing rules. In his answer, Jesus pointed out that these were traditional regulations developed by men, but far more serious were the violations of biblical regulations that the religious leaders themselves committed. He took as his example the commandment to honour father and mother. This required much greater commitment than handwash-ing; it included personal cost in offering financial and other support to parents. Yet these unscrupulous lead-ers (no doubt with clean hands) had found a way round those obligations. A simple declaration that all their pos-sessions or savings were a gift to God and especially ded-icated to him could swiftly justify their claim that these resources were unavailable to help their parents. Dick France spells it out bluntly:

This convenient declaration apparently left the property actually still at the disposal of the one who made the vow but deprived his parents of any right to it . . . Such a pious fraud is in direct conflict with the will of God expressed in the fifth commandment.[1]

The mask of ultra-religiosity may have been crafted to hide the violation from the people, but it was not hidden from Jesus. He spelled out how they twisted the law and revealed their double-mindedness (15.1–9). Even more, he identified them as those about whom Isaiah had prophesied.

Hypocrites! Well did Isaiah prophesy about you, saying:

'These people draw near to Me with their mouth,
And honor Me with their lips,
But their heart is far from Me.
And in vain they worship Me,
Teaching as doctrines the commandments of
   men.'
(Matthew 15.7–9, NKJV)

The fulfilment quotation here certainly hit its mark. Matthew does not record any verbal response from the scribes and Pharisees, quite possibly because there wasn't one. With lip service unveiled and heart service found wanting, justification was hard to find.

The quotation from Isaiah does open up another aspect of Jesus' teaching important in Matthew's Gospel: the biblical doctrine of the heart. 'Heart' is used more than 700 times in Scripture. It refers to the very core of a person. It is where our will, our attitudes, decisions and intentions have their source. We choose from our heart and believe in our heart. 'The fool says in his heart [not his mind], "There is no God"' (Psalm 14.1).

Jesus shows that the priorities we have, the values we hold, are largely directed by our heart. 'For where your treasure is, there your heart will be also' (Matthew 6.21). He asks us to set our hearts on what is good. It is the 'pure in heart' who will see God (5.8). Conversely, if the heart is corrupted it can be seen in our lies and distortions: 'what comes out of the mouth proceeds from the heart, and this is what defiles' (15.18, NRSV). A corrupted heart spreads malice: 'the mouth speaks what the heart is full of' (12.34). It produces evil at the very centre of our being: 'out of the heart come evil thoughts – murder, adultery, sexual immorality, theft, false testimony, slander. These are what defile a person' (15.19–20). So the idea that we can solve the problems of sin by sanitizing our hands or following ablution rituals is bizarre. They can do nothing to eradicate attitudes deeply seated in the heart. Jesus' warning to both his disciples and the crowds is to guard their hearts carefully. They must also avoid 'blind guides', who elevate human traditions and turn them into biblical commandments. Today, Jesus' distinction between lip service and heart service towards God still challenges us. Whatever our culture, we understand people so much better when we have a biblical understanding of 'heart'.

On the road to Jerusalem, one of the tasks for Jesus was to draw vulnerable people away from imposed rituals into the heart commitments that characterized kingdom living.

But he faced opposition. The closer he got to Jerusalem, the more his opponents tested him. Matthew records one example of this on the issue of divorce.

Marriage and divorce

Matthew had already briefly reported Jesus' teaching on divorce back in Galilee (5.31–32). Now, the Pharisees in Judea followed it up with a question concerning divorce and the law: 'Is it lawful for a man to divorce his wife for any and every reason?' (19.3). Their question sounds innocent enough. Matthew makes it clear to us that it was not. Far from offering an invitation to a normal rabbinical discussion, with honest theological exchanges, he says the intention was to test Jesus. It is significant that the word Matthew uses here for 'test' is the same one he used when he wrote of the temptations from the devil. To the Pharisees, however, it offered the real possibility of embroiling Jesus in controversy. Divorce was a hot topic and it shouldn't have been difficult to find some legal point to use as a lever against him.

In the Jewish community a polarizing debate had developed around the proper grounds for divorce. Everyone knew that the Mosaic Law permitted divorce as spelled out in Deuteronomy 24.1–4. It specified that if a man married a woman and she found no favour in his eyes because of some fault (or 'uncleanness') in her, he may give her a bill of divorce and send her away. The rabbinical debate centred on what constituted the 'fault' or 'uncleanness'. Rabbi Shammai and his school took a firm view, limiting its meaning to adultery/fornication only. Rabbi Hillel and his school followed a more flexible interpretation, maintaining that it could apply to any 'fault' in the wife, such as irritability, talking to strangers or burning the food. So, effectively, the Pharisees were asking Jesus to judge between these major positions. It might have sounded like the typical rabbinic debate, but for Matthew the objective was clear. Whichever side Jesus took on the legality or grounds for divorce, he would make new enemies.

Jesus' response was to refuse to answer their purported legal dilemma. Instead, he addressed the underlying meaning of marriage and relationships. He challenged them on their reading of Genesis, reiterating the point that God made people male and female, and that in marriage we become 'one flesh'. The picture he offered was of the creation of a loving intimacy between two partners – sexual, emotional and spiritual – so deep that the couple enjoys a form of bodily and spiritual union. Given that this is God's will and intention 'what God has joined together, let no one separate' (19.6).

The Pharisees tried again, implying that Jesus was contradicting the Mosaic Law: why then had Moses commanded that they give a bill of divorce? The question was loaded and the implication false. The bill of divorce was by no means a *command* of law but a concession. Jesus answered that it was because of men's hardness of heart. He was not allowing them to elevate a concession provided because of sin into a divine command. Instead he referred them back to the beginning. He repeated his teaching on the Sermon on the Mount (5.31–32), stating categorically: 'Moses permitted you to divorce your wives because your hearts were hard. But it was not this way from the beginning. I tell you that any-one who divorces his wife, except for sexual immorality, and marries another woman commits adultery' (19.8–9).

Matthew implicitly puts what Jesus says here on a par with his other statements of 'You have heard that it was said . . . but I say to you . . .'. Again, he interprets the law as being more demanding than the superficial observance given to it. Here he is suggesting that, rather than requiring a man to give a bill of divorce, there should be no divorce at all except where there is adultery.[2] The deep meaning of marital union had higher requirements than issuing a bill.

Jesus' teaching has often been seen in Christian circles today as largely reinforcing a prohibitionist view of divorce, but it is more radical and complex than that. The issue is more nuanced when we take it out of its historical and cultural context and apply it today. To understand this, we need to look at the context more fully.

Israel was a patriarchal society, and the provisions for divorce made by the Mosaic Law, and in all the courts and councils, were provisions designed and delivered for men. The debate between the schools of Shammai and Hillel did not address the issue about women divorcing their husbands for a very good reason. Quite simply, there was no such issue. Only the man could take the steps required for a valid Jewish divorce; he could not be divorced by his wife, for she had no power of petition.

Inevitably, this increased the power of the husband and the vulnerability of the wife: a married woman had little recourse if she was badly treated, and she could be dismissed from the marriage without any consultation and against her will. The 'bill of divorce' was a minor legal protection in two small ways. It was a delaying mechanism. The husband was required to write such a bill and present it to her before sending her away. It meant that although he could threaten divorce in a fit of anger, he could not carry it out with validity until the bill was presented to her.[3] It meant also that the woman had some legal status as a divorcee: she did not remain technically married to him while at the same time he abandoned her. But this was still a provision that suited the man more than the woman. Divorce was still enacted on the unilateral declaration of the husband; the wife still had no appeal she could lodge, nor legal entitlement to any settlement.

In his comeback to the Pharisees Jesus is clearly addressing the men. They are the only ones who matter, for the law refers to them. And he is making it clear that Moses' provision for them was only because of the hardness of their hearts. Was it right that if a man had tired of his wife, or decided he wanted to replace her, she could be legally disposed of? No, says Jesus. This was hard-heartedness, giving legal approval to men's lack of care and compassion. It was condoning their readiness to break the marital bond as stated in Genesis. Morally and spiritually, a wife should not be treated this way. Only if she herself has committed adultery does the man have any case for divorce to be sanctioned. Otherwise, however religious and law-abiding a man thinks he is, disposing of a wife and taking another simply makes him an adulterer.

Jesus' response to the Pharisees is a radical upholding of God's plan for marriage. He reinstates its originally intended meaning. It can certainly be seen as an implicit plea for married people to love one other more; to show sensitivity, concern and respect for each other; to work out their grievances when they occur and forgive each other's failings. But it is also an acknowledgement of the vulnerability of women in a culture where men made all the decisions. It could even be seen as an attack on the one-sidedness of divorce. I suspect the Pharisees got the point: a man should not be allowed the level of power that could leave a woman destitute and isolated if her husband simply wanted a change. They were probably startled by his answer. But if they had understood Jesus' identification with people who were marginalized by their culture, they would have been less so. For it was in keeping with the many ways Jesus showed consideration and appreciation towards women. Luke's Gospel emphasizes this even more, but Matthew also brings it out in Jesus' encounter with the Canaanite woman (15.21–28) and his anointing at Bethany (26.6–13). He shows us Jesus was clearly ready to undermine the entrenched patterns of disregard for women in patriarchal culture. As feminist theologian Rosemary Radford Ruether points out:

The Gospel returns us to the world of Pharisees and priests, widows and prostitutes, homeless Jewish prophets and Syro-Phoenician women. Men and women interact with each other within a multiplicity of social definitions: sexual status, but also ethnicity, social class, religious office and law define relations with each other. Jesus as liberator calls for a renunciation and dissolution of this web of status relationships by which societies have defined privilege and unprivilege. He speaks especially to outcast women, not as representatives of the 'feminine', but because they are at the bottom of this network of oppression. His ability to be liberator does not reside in his maleness, but, on the contrary, in the fact that he has renounced this system of domination and seeks to embody in his person the new humanity of service and mutual empowerment.[4]

His disciples certainly recognized the restraints Jesus was putting on men and their rights with regard to divorce. Their suggestion that it might be better not to marry, then, may have been banter, but Jesus used it to agree that marriage is demanding and brings responsibilities that should not be evaded. At the same time, Jesus acknowledged that not all are called to be married. People remain celibate for many different reasons and that is also a calling before God.

The rich young man

Not all of those who came to Jesus with a question were trying to trap him. The rich young man came with a genuine spiritual issue. What good deed must he do to gain eternal life (19.16–22)? There were two assumptions wrapped up in his question. The first was that eternal life is somehow related to our 'doing' and not our 'being'. The second was that some good deeds bring us higher credit with God than others, so what could these be?

Jesus immediately addresses the philosophical issue relating to his concept of 'good'. Goodness cannot be defined by our activity; it is not the property of human beings. God alone is good, so goodness can only be found in reflecting God and keeping the commandments that emanate from God. Jesus specifies the commandments that show us how to live in neighbourly love and the young man feels he has kept all these. Yet he realizes they are not enough. Jesus' final response, telling him, then, to sell all he has, give his money to the poor and follow him, lands as a huge blow. Matthew tells us that the young man went away sorrowful, for his possessions were considerable.

The young man is probably archetypal of many God-seekers. He has both sincerity and discernment. He knows that he falls short. He wants to change in order to gain eternal life. Yet when Jesus pinpoints where change is needed, the cost becomes too great. Jesus does not make discipleship easy – it's hard.

Most of us can see the problematic relationship between wealth and the kingdom of heaven. Jesus' exaggerated simile says it all. The camel was probably the largest animal the disciples had seen and the idea of it passing through the eye of a needle was absurd. But why is it difficult for a rich man to enter heaven? And does it apply to all rich people? Even the disciples are thrown by Jesus' comparison – if those whom God has already blessed with riches can't enter the kingdom of heaven, who can? Peter examines their own credentials and points out that they have given up everything to follow Jesus.

It is a pertinent issue for the disciples, and possibly for some of us. For Peter might well protest that they had relinquished everything, but we know he had a substantial house that accommodated his mother-in-law and was where Jesus often lived (8.14–15). Other followers of Jesus also had possessions, not least Levi, who showed hospitality. So weren't these double standards?

The answer is no. It was not wealth in and of itself that barred entry to the kingdom of heaven, but the place it had in someone's life. For the young man it was central; to give it all up, become poor, itinerant, vulnerable and dependent on others, was something he could not bear to consider. But possessions were not important for any of Jesus' followers. They never (other than for Judas) got in the way of commitment and service. Fully available to Jesus, the disciples had, in effect, renounced their goods; possessions were merely functional – resources to be used for the kingdom and not idols for worship. And Jesus affirmed that his disciples, along with all those who renounced the world for his sake, would indeed be with him in the kingdom.

The parable of the vineyard owner

Having ended his discussion on wealth with the epigrammatic point that 'many who are first will be last, and many who are last will be first', Jesus then produces a parable about workers in a vineyard to illustrate the upside-down values of the kingdom. He picks up the refrain of the earlier kingdom parables (13.1–52), 'The kingdom of heaven is like . . .', and this time the main focus is a landowner who needs workers for his vineyard.

The vineyard owner goes out early in the morning to where labourers congregate, selects his workforce and makes a contract with them for the usual daily wage. Three hours later, he goes back to the marketplace and takes on more workers, promising to pay them what is right. Three hours later at noon, and then at three in the afternoon, he goes again to the marketplace and hires yet more labourers. Finally, one hour before the end of the day, he returns to the marketplace and finds men still hanging around. He asks why they have been *idle* all day – a word with strong resonances in our own contemporary society, summing up negative attitudes to unemployed people. Their answer is also resonant today: they haven't found anyone to take them on. So with no contract, and no promise of any rate of pay, the landowner sends them too into the vineyard to work. One hour later, work ends and the vineyard owner delegates the manager to call and pay the workers, beginning with the ones hired last.

Seeing that the labourers hired last for one hour had received the whole of a daily wage, the ones hired first expected a bonanza. Unsurprisingly, they were very put out when everyone received the same wage irrespective of hours worked. Equal pay for unequal work must have seemed unfair to those who had done most of it! However, their complaint – 'You have made them equal to us who have borne the burden of the work and heat of the day' – cut no ice with the landowner. He argued that he had done them no wrong, paid the contractual wage already agreed, but had chosen to be generous to the others. His generosity ought not to be a cause for envy. Then Jesus repeats that the last will be first and the first will be last.

It's a wonderfully rich parable. Many have interpreted it to be about salvation: eleventh-hour, death-bed conversions.

Those who entered the vineyard at the very end of the day got the same wages as those who had worked all day; those who respond to the word of God at the end of life are welcomed into the kingdom on the same basis as those who have spent a lifetime in God's service. It's a salvation principle.

A second interpretation points to the difference between grace and law. Those who came first were contracted on a legal basis with an agreed daily rate, paid on conclusion of the work. They worked under the law and were paid according to the law. Those who had no contract and were ushered into the vineyard without promises had only the mercy of the landowner to rely on. But they were shown grace, more powerful than law, and received what they did not deserve.

A third theme is that of Jews and Gentiles. The Jews are the ones who have served God through history, honouring the covenant, bearing the heat and struggles of being God's people. The Gentiles are the Johnny-come-latelies who have not had the onus of obeying the Law and the Prophets. But God invites them too and they are received into the kingdom of heaven with no differentials between them and the Jews.

The final interpretation concerns justice and mercy. Those picked first are the ones who are in the right place to work the system and negotiate a contract. Those employed at the end of the day are the marginalized and the infirm: the global poor, the disenfranchised and those with no voices. But they still have families to feed and people to care for, so they will work for whatever they can get. In the kingdoms of this world they will be exploited. The owners of corporate capital can move from region to region to find the cheapest workforce and lowest tax rates and thus accumulate the highest profits. These vulnerable unhired labourers are desperate and at risk. But the vineyard owner does not exploit. He gives from his own generosity to ensure that there are no poor. And Jesus says that the kingdom of heaven is like this landowner.

In all these interpretations, Jesus paints a wonderful, inclusive, generous picture of the one who rules in the kingdom of heaven. He concludes with the statement he made before the parable – that the first will be last and the last first. This is not, however, simply the order in which people were paid, but also the way the world's values are turned upside down in the kingdom of heaven. It also refers to the end of a race. When the first comes last and the last comes first, you have a dead heat. Their timing is identical. And so once again we see in Jesus' parable a wonderful egalitarian picture of the kingdom of heaven.

Jesus prepares the disciples

The disciples clearly enjoyed Jesus' parables. They may not have enjoyed his reminders of what lay ahead. Twice already Jesus had told his disciples about the outcome of the journey. He had explained that he must go to Jerusalem and 'suffer many things at the hands of the elders, the chief priests and the teachers of the law' (16.21). Peter's attempt to dissuade him simply produced a sharp rebuke from Jesus, for bringing temptation from Satan. On a second occasion Jesus told them about the impending betrayal: that he would be delivered into the hands of people who would kill him, and he would be raised on the third day (17.22–23). Again, the disciples were greatly distressed. Now, for a third time, Jesus spells out what awaits them:

> 'We are going up to Jerusalem, and the Son of Man will be delivered over to the chief priests and the teachers of the law. They will condemn him to death and will hand him over to the Gentiles to be mocked and flogged and crucified. On the third day he will be raised to life.' (20.17–19)

Note that there is no uncertainty here in what Jesus says. He is not warning them that this could happen in a worst-case scenario. He is absolutely clear what will transpire and wants his disciples to know. And they, having been fore-warned of persecution, floggings and trials from the beginning of their time with him (10.16–23), now know that these things are not far off.

In Luke's Gospel the sons of Zebedee are even hasti-er in their response than Peter had been. They ask Jesus if he wants them to call fire down from heaven to consume the opposition (Luke 9.54). Jesus certainly does not; it is the opposite of what he is asking of his disciples. But their question raises an important issue:

> Here is a question put to every believer by this text: does discipleship mean deploying God's missiles against the enemy in righteous indignation? Or does discipleship mean following him on the Calvary road which leads

to suffering and death? The answer of the whole New Testament is . . . that it demands a life of sacrificial, dying service before we can reign with Christ in glory.[5]

Some years ago I was speaking at a large ecumenical gathering in Amsterdam, sharing accommodation with other speakers from across the world. One of my breakfast partners was a Dutch Catholic priest in his early forties who had served in many parts of the world where poverty and disease were rampant. He was enjoying a brief spell in the Netherlands after many years abroad. On the final morning he came down to breakfast with an expression on his face that I didn't recognize. I asked him if everything was OK. He affirmed that it was but he had just received news of his next posting. He was to serve in Somalia. 'How long will you be there?' I asked. 'Oh, until I die,' was the reply. I began to smile before I realized he was completely serious. He went on to explain that the work in that region required people who were prepared to be martyred, because that was usually their fate. He had been selected to replace a brother from his Order who had just been murdered. He smiled and said, 'There is no date for any return journey. But that is always the case when God calls you to serve him.' After a few moments of silence as I processed what he had just told me, we prayed together, and then he went to prepare for his travels to Africa. As he walked quietly away, I was left pensive and challenged by his calmness and peace.

It is not always easy to understand why Christians are persecuted. But it is almost always associated with their stand of obedience to Christ. There is something about a Christian refusal, whether that is a refusal to lie, to hit back in anger or to compromise, that unnerves those opposed to the Gospel. Sometimes, it wins opponents over and a level of reconciliation becomes possible. More often it hardens their resolve to attack and undermine those whose commitment they cannot abide.

Jesus knew well the trauma that awaited him in Jerusalem, and calling down fire from heaven was not on his agenda. He knew the outcome of anger towards him would result in his crucifixion, but he knew also that the good news of the kingdom of God would spread beyond the confines of Israel and draw in people from every nation. His own resolution to stay faithful and face the cost of his calling has been the bedrock of assurance for so many who have followed him on a journey to death.

The mother of the sons of Zebedee

Jesus' warnings about suffering and death clearly raised many questions for the disciples. It was inevitable that his followers would want to know what it would be like for them. Among his travelling party were the women who had been supporting Jesus and his disciples in Galilee. Some of them are named in the Gospel of Luke (8), and Matthew names others himself. One of them remains unnamed in all the Gospels and is known only by her title: the 'mother of the sons of Zebedee'. Clearly her connection with Jesus' disciples James and John was more public than her role as Zebedee's wife. She comes to Jesus to ask if her sons may sit on Jesus' right and left hand in the kingdom. It is a curious request and angers the other disciples. It does not anger Jesus. He simply points out what is entailed. Are they prepared for the suffering that he will have to undertake first? Are they able to 'drink his cup'? James and John say they are. Jesus confirms that they will indeed undergo suffering, yet he cannot make promises to them about the future. That is the province of the Father alone. The conversation that follows with the disciples is not a rebuke of the mother of James and John but a reinforcement of all his teaching on servant leadership. To be great is to serve, not to lord it over one another. And in the principle of servant leadership another mark of the kingdom of heaven is firmly established.

The mother of the sons of Zebedee has been somewhat scorned by commentators as a social climber, wanting special privileges for her sons. There may well have been an element of that in her request to Jesus. But she was a mother. Her desire was clearly that her sons would remain close to Jesus, whom they loved and served, in whatever they encountered. That was not only their privilege, it was also their protection. She was a faithful believer who had not only given her sons up to be Jesus' disciples but had herself become part of the travelling group of supporters. She, along with Mary Magdalene, Joanna and other women followers, had travelled with Jesus on this epic journey from Galilee to Jerusalem to 'care for his needs'. At the very end, when all of Jesus' predictions about his fate have been proved true, Matthew reminds us again of this mother of the sons of Zebedee. She is among those who remain near the cross, watching in distress as Jesus dies. With the other women she will also emulate Jesus' servanthood in going to anoint his body, but instead will be one of the witnesses to his glorious resurrection.

The healing of two men who were blind

As they come within reach of Jerusalem, Matthew records another miracle. Two men sitting by the roadside share one debilitating feature – their lack of sight. The crowd show no interest in their condition and simply ask them to be quiet when they shout to get Jesus' attention. The men have obviously heard the crowd's acclamation and call out to him themselves, 'Lord, Son of David, have mercy on us.' Their plea is for Israel's Messiah to show compassion and mercy to two men without sight. Matthew tells us that compassion moved Jesus and he healed them. Without any further invitation they followed him.

It is a story that prepares us for Jesus' entry into Jerusalem. The crowds are convinced: the sick are healed and the blind see. Many have been on the road with Jesus from Galilee, as it is Passover time; they have heard his teaching and seen his authority. Pilgrims are descending on Jerusalem from all parts of the country; they too will acknowledge him. It is indeed the time to announce the Messiah, to crown the King.

The triumphal entry into Jerusalem

Jesus and his disciples had walked all the way from Galilee. Walking was their normal mode of transport, so it would have been perfectly easy for them all to complete the last two miles into Jerusalem on foot. But from chapter 16, Matthew has been preparing us for a climactic entry and a symbolic fulfilment of prophecy. Jesus sends his disciples to bring him a donkey and her foal, in what seems to have been a prearranged agreement with the owner. Jesus was to mount the foal that had never been ridden, so it was an act of animal kindness that its mother should come too. Matthew comments with a 'fulfilment quotation' from Zechariah 9.9:

> This took place to fulfil what had been spoken through the prophet:
>
> 'Say to Daughter Zion,
> "See, your king comes to you,
> gentle and riding on a donkey,
> and on a colt, the foal of a donkey."'
> (21.4–5)[6]

Seated on the foal, Jesus rides into Jerusalem. The prophecy yields an insight into the kind of king that Israel ought to be expecting, one that Jesus readily accepted. Its nonconformity to the values of the world has struck many people:

> Riding the donkey, he rejected both the reality and the trappings of power. This king-on-a-donkey refused to conform to the expected image, the accepted values of the society of his time. He came humbly, choosing the

way of peace, relying on the quiet persistence of love, rather than the sterile forces of compulsion.[7]

Jesus' act was not to show a messiah of force and might, but a messiah who would undergo suffering. Yet the crowds were not to know that as they greeted him with shouts of 'Hosanna!' (save us). Their obeisance, throwing cloaks on the road and branches cut from the trees, was in keeping with their conviction that this indeed was the son of David, come in the name of the Lord. The image foreseen by Zechariah took life among the people; the claim to messiahship was now supported symbolically by Jesus himself. And Matthew tells us that, as he entered Jerusalem, the whole city was stirred.

What were the people's expectations? What would happen next? No one ponders this more vividly than Spurgeon:

Had it been our Lord's will, those multitudes who followed him in the streets would actually have crowned him there and then, and bowing the knee, they would have accepted him as the branch that sprung out of the dried root of Jesse . . . the ruler, the Shiloh among God's people. He had only to have said a word, and they would have rushed with him at their head to Pilate's palace, and taking him by surprise, with but few soldiers in the land, Pilate might soon have been his prisoner, and have been tried for his life. Before the indomitable valour and the tremendous fury of a Jewish army, Palestine might soon have been cleared of all the Roman legions, and have become again a royal land.[8]

But this was not the Lord's will. God's kingdom way is different. With the end of the journey to Jerusalem came the start of the intense ordeal Jesus had to suffer. It would ultimately result in victory over evil. But first, wrongs had to be addressed and warnings given. And Jesus knew the cost.

5

Meeting God in woes
and warnings

Matthew is clear about what follows Jesus' spectacular entry into the city. Others, unfamiliar with the development of his Gospel, might not be. A few years ago I was in the Yorkshire Dales as a 'visiting theologian' and had just gone through the events of Palm Sunday with children in a primary school. I asked them what they thought Jesus might do after he got into Jerusalem. One hand shot up immediately. A very practical seven-year-old had the answer: 'He would tell one of his disciples to take the donkeys back.'

Matthew doesn't give us any further information on the donkeys, but he does change the scene away from the enthusiasm of the crowd and the cries of 'Hosanna!' We are shown a contrast to Jesus' teaching on the kingdom of heaven, with his challenging stories of precious pearls and mustard seeds, growing wheat and catching fish. It's also a contrast to his 'comfortable words', which come as precious balm to tired souls, when worries weigh us down: 'Come to me, all you who are weary and burdened, and I will give you rest. Take my yoke upon you and learn from me, for I am gentle and humble in heart, and you will find rest for your souls' (11.28–30). Now Matthew discloses in one outstanding illustration what Jesus has been teaching *against*:

the sham living, the distortions of justice and the worship of Mammon. These all confront Jesus as he moves swiftly into a public reckoning in the Temple.

Overturning the money tables

Herod's Temple was an enormous renovation of the original Second Temple, with the base of the Temple extended by a massive retaining wall. Around the Temple courts a large amount of economic activity took place, especially just before festival time. Money-changers exchanged foreign coins for Jewish money, the only currency used in Jerusalem. Animals for sacrifice were sold, as it was easier for pilgrims to buy them there than to bring them on the long journey. Animals that had been brought for sacrifice were examined by officials to determine whether they were acceptable. All of this involved money changing hands.

The account of Jesus overturning the money tables is the only physically aggressive act by Jesus recorded in the Gospels. It is often misunderstood as something spurred by sudden, out-of-control anger, but the Gospels suggest it was a planned action. It was also more than outrage against corruption and fair exchange distorted by theft. He does not seem to have been railing primarily against exploitation of the poor, nor objecting to abuse of foreigners, strictly forbidden in the Mosaic Law (Exodus 22.21; Leviticus 19.33–34). The traders may well have been taking advantage of their privileged position and lining their own pockets, but the rebuke was also aimed at those who were buying. Jesus' action was an attack on the whole enterprise, the way in which buying and selling of animals for sacrificial worship had grown into big business. It had usurped the Temple's identity as a place where God alone was worshipped; these economic priorities were now making clear that the actual focus of this worship was Mammon.

Jesus' wrath was not only against those involved in overt financial dealings. It was against the Temple's authorities too. The money-changers, the traders and officials conducting business would not have been there without their permission. Once again, those on the receiving end of Jesus' reprimands were religious leaders whose calling to bless and release people seeking God had got lost somewhere. Their legalism allowed them to try to get the 'specks' out of the eyes of others while ignoring the great 'logs' in their own (7.4). Jesus now indicted them for hypocrisy and willingly colluding with the traders to turn God's house of prayer into a den of thieves (21.12–13).

Though this action is dramatic, it reflects many warnings Jesus has given. Long before this confrontation with idolatry Jesus had been publicly admonishing the rejection of God's truth in towns and cities where the power of God had been witnessed, yet people had not repented. So 'woe' was pronounced on the lakeside towns of Chorazin and Bethsaida because their people had disregarded God's word. 'Woe' was also declared on Capernaum, a much more significant city, where there was no penitence for wrong, despite Jesus' teaching and healing. When Jesus compared these places unfavourably with the towns under judgement in the Old Testament – Tyre, Sidon and Sodom – Matthew knew his readers would get the point (11.20–24).

The Temple showed the juxtaposition of idolatry and humble belief. Those worshipping Mammon showed anger towards Jesus, especially religious leaders who had not served the people and been exposed. The fruitlessness of their ministry was symbolically reflected in the incident of the barren fig tree, which had its 'ministry' removed by Jesus (21.18–22). Yet the humble ones flocked to Jesus for healing and comfort – even young children shouted 'Hosanna'. The impact of this did not bring any conviction of wrongdoing to the religious authorities. Instead, a high-level deputation, which included some from the Sanhedrin, came to question Jesus about where his authority came from. Jesus refused to answer and asked them instead where John's baptism came from. Realizing that their question had backfired and that whatever answer they gave would bring them enemies, his adversaries ended the conversation (21.27).

Three parables

Jesus' priority was not to win arguments over the Sanhedrin or chief priests, but to reach the crowds with his teaching. Once again he told parables, allowing his hearers to work out the meaning and application for themselves. Now his theme was obedience and disobedience towards God.

In the parable of the two sons, one son refuses a request from his father but later does it; the other son accepts the request but then ignores it. Jesus' point is that what counts is not verbal promise, but actual delivery. The leaders are implicitly identified as the disobedient son, while tax collectors and prostitutes, whom the Pharisees despise, are identified as the obedient one; having heard the preaching of John the Baptist, they have changed their minds and repented, unlike the Pharisees. They will go before the religious leaders into the kingdom of heaven.

Two more parables, those of the wicked tenants and the wedding banquet, continue the ongoing dialogue with his opponents. In each of them, Jesus sketches allegorically Israel's oppressive treatment of God's prophets, and finally their rejection of God's Son. The solemn ending of the parables is that both the wicked tenants and those declining to attend the wedding banquet receive dramatic punishment. The parables also forecast clearly that the spiritual heritage will be taken from those who abuse it and given to others who produce the fruits of the kingdom (21.23 – 22.14).

Three questions

Matthew then moves us from parables to questions, and in the first, rabbinic students are sent to Jesus to ask a question about taxation (22.15–23). Imperial taxes were a great bone of contention, for they were levied by the Roman overlords in collusion with Jewish tax collectors, who did their bidding and profited themselves. Anger at this taxation simmered among Jewish nationalists and Zealot resistance movements, fuelled by the memory of a revolt in AD 6. So the question 'Is it lawful to pay taxes to the emperor?' was an unexploded bomb, which they hoped might be ignited among either his Jewish followers or the Roman authorities, depending on Jesus' answer. Jesus saw their insincerity and side-stepped the issue with a question about whose head was on a coin. When the answer was 'Caesar's', Jesus' instruction cut swiftly through their subterfuge: 'Give back to Caesar what is Caesar's and to God what is God's' (22.21).

Some people have heard in this response a 'secular–sacred dualism'. They argue that Jesus was reinforcing a division in society between politics and religion, insisting that they should always be kept separate. But we can easily see he was not. Instead, he was laying down two very important principles about secular authority: its legitimacy and its boundaries. He intended his audience to understand that although political authority has legitimacy, it should never be totalitarian or absolute. Even Caesar, for all his political might, had very limited jurisdiction (reflected, incidentally, in that the coin bearing his head was a tiny denarius!). God, however, is sovereign over everything. So, if Caesar was justly entitled to taxes (and thereby hung a question), people should pay their taxes. But to give to God what belongs to God involves surrendering all we have, because God requires total allegiance.

The next question was from the Sadducees about a seven-times-married widow: whose wife would she be in the 'resurrection'? Recognizing this as a typical way of ridiculing belief in the resurrection, Jesus moved in on their problem of unbelief and challenged their assumption that resurrection life was like that on earth (22.23–33). The fact that God is the God of the living indicates instead that new life lies beyond the grave.

In answer to the third question, from a Pharisee asking Jesus to specify the greatest commandment, he again diverted the focus, refusing to engage with obsessive debates over ranking laws. He answered simply, "'Love the Lord your God with all your heart and with all your soul and with all your mind." This is the first and greatest commandment.' Adding a summary of all the other Commandments, 'Love your neighbour as yourself', Jesus affirmed these as the bedrock on which all the other teachings hang (22.34–40).

The questions were hostile, but Jesus used them as an opportunity for teaching. Matthew reports that the people in the crowd, who were bystanders to the exchanges were astounded at his replies. When Jesus finally put his own question to the Pharisees, about the identity of the Messiah, he cogently argued from Scripture that he was both the son of David and the Lord of David. Like an exhausted and defeated prosecutor in a law court, his interrogators then had no further questions.

Confrontations with the scribes and Pharisees (Matthew 23.1–29)

Throughout the Gospel, Matthew has followed the confrontation between Jesus and the religious teachers. It now reaches its climax in chapter 23. First Jesus assures his disciples and the crowds that he is not questioning the legitimate authority of the religious leaders. They are commissioned to teach the Law of Moses, so people should listen, but the hearers should not follow their warped practices. Jesus identifies two deep failings that often go together: hypocrisy and spiritual blindness. These failings are not a simple matter of the mind or understanding, and certainly not one of ritual, but of the heart. Jesus warns against motives that reek of insincerity and are driven by pride and vanity rather than humble service. The religious leaders put heavy legalistic burdens on people who seek God, multiplying the ways they can offend God. They seek adulation and praise; they want to be seen and applauded by other people. Even their clothes and apparatus are ostentatious. Status, prestige, pride and entitlement dominate the way they relate to those searching for God, and Jesus pronounces judgement on them.

When Jesus focuses his teaching on his disciples, we see the radical contrast of this to the outlook of the Pharisees. He offers a completely different way of exercising leadership, which breaks free entirely from Pharisaic legalism. It is egalitarian and entirely unconventional. No hierarchy is displayed here; no one gets any title, all are students, all are learning from the one teacher, the Messiah. Jesus unobtrusively claims that unique title. In asserting his own authority, Jesus takes it away from everyone else. But the leadership Jesus offers is servant leadership, by which his followers must be moulded.

Like all kingdom values, servant leadership is profoundly different from rivalry and control. It runs counter to the way the world understands status, and challenges the way power imposes burdens on others. Jesus continually reminded his listeners that all we do has consequences; wrongs can leave a legacy of pain that can seep down through generations. Leadership exercised in the kingdom way can release people from the past and help them to experience the renewing power of the Holy Spirit. It works within the whole body of Christ, where we learn from God together, discern together and are given gifts in the body to be used for the kingdom of heaven. Leaders who lead in this way are not wanting us to admire their own wisdom, but through their prayer and spiritual insight they help us into a deeper encounter with God. Although a faithful Jew, Jesus was not in the business of promoting religion. His leadership urged people to hear the good news of the kingdom of heaven and live it out in their ordinary everyday lives.

The contrast between holding on to power to benefit self and using power to serve others has been apparent in every era throughout history. Lauding it over others can never sit together with seeking the common good. So, the greatest is the one who serves. Those who put themselves above others will be brought down, while the humble are elevated. Theirs is the spirit we need to emulate. Matthew makes it easy for us to understand Jesus' reproaches towards the religious authorities of his day.

The seven woes (23.13–36)

When Jesus finally addresses the scribes and Pharisees themselves, it is to confront them with their failures as divinely appointed guides of Israel. Jesus outlines these failures in seven 'woes', all but one introduced by the phrase 'Woe to you, teachers of the law and Pharisees, you hypocrites . . .'.

A woe is something heavier than a lament. It's not even the same as 'Whoa!' – our caution meaning 'Stop, hold on there!' The word used in Matthew's Gospel (and in Luke 11) combines a cry of danger and denunciation. It draws attention to something so bad that it can no longer be ignored.

We can compare the seven woes with the eight Beatitudes earlier in the Gospel, for in many ways they are polar opposites, both in attitude and resulting lifestyle. In the Beatitudes Jesus celebrates with joy those who are blessed; in the woes he shouts in distress at those who corrupt the faith. And each of the seven woes pinpoints an aspect of hypocrisy or faithlessness in leadership that Jesus now holds up to judgement.

Related themes are interwoven through these woes. And though the language reflects the religious cultures and practices of his hearers, and identifies key failings of leadership then, the principles behind them do speak into our situation today. Let me try to summarize briefly the accusations Jesus raised against the leaders.

1 They made it hard for other people to receive salvation and understand true teaching, having rejected it themselves.
2 They chased after converts but misled them about real belief, effectively turning them into unbelievers.
3 They trivialized faith by constructing pointless debates about oaths, distorting values and meanings.
4 They demonstrated entirely wrong priorities – tithing inconsequential items like mint, dill and cumin while ignoring big issues like justice, mercy and faithfulness.
5 They operated superficial observance (for example, of ablution laws) to keep up appearances, but ignored the contaminating grime and dirt beneath.
6 They covered up their wrong, deep-seated mindsets and practices with false piety so people would not see their hypocrisy.

7 They resembled, in all their attitudes, arrogance and inher-
itance, those who killed the prophets and messengers from
God.

That last woe was far-reaching and touched into the long
history of Israel's failure as God's people. It also offered
predictions for the future. Of the messengers God was now
sending, some would be flogged in the synagogues, and
some persecuted and crucified – a clear reference to both Jesus and his disciples. The underlying message, now brought
out so very clearly, was that 'Jesus' own generation is the one
in which Jewish rebellion against God reaches its climax
and will therefore incur its ultimate punishment'.[1]

The seven woes present a formidable list of failures and
distortions of true faith with uncompromising words
and graphic, unforgettable pictures. The reference to the
'brood of vipers' takes us back to Matthew's account of John
the Baptist, who had been sent to warn the people and tell
them of the coming of the kingdom. The reference to 'whitewashed tombs' conjures up an image of containers for bones
(ossuaries) beautified with plaster of marble and lime, but
inside containing the stench of death. Such comparisons
were hard-hitting and unlikely to appease the teachers of
the law and the Pharisees. But Jesus saw no point in offering compromise. He knew the future. His opponents must
be told the truth.

It was inevitable that Jesus' focus would eventually turn
to Jerusalem. It was not simply because of the leaders who
had turned away from God and killed the prophets; Jesus
also saw Jerusalem as symbolizing all of Israel being under

judgement from God. Hypocrisy, untruth and wrongdoing had embedded themselves into national as well as personal life. When condoned they become part of a cultural mindset that is normalized and thereby much harder to resist.

So Jesus' woes became a lament and brought dire warning of future shock, with predictions that signified great catastrophe. He expressed poignant motherly longing, presenting himself as a hen longing to gather her chicks to safety under her wings. His longing was for Israel's repentance so that the punishment and devastation could be averted. His lament was that such repentance had not come. It is an echo of the pain of Jeremiah, weeping over Jerusalem:

Since my people are crushed, I am crushed;
I mourn, and horror grips me.
Is there no balm in Gilead?
Is there no physician there?
Why then is there no healing
for the wound of my people?
(Jeremiah 8.21–22)

The pain was for all Israel, but Jerusalem and its Temple would know the catastrophe most severely.

Woes to our generation?

Though our context is so different, it is sobering to ask what woes Jesus might bring today to those of us who profess religious faith. Certainly, we have judgementalism in the Church and a failure to see our own faults.

Certainly, religious hypocrisy exists where the desire to be well thought of by others is greater than the desire to serve God with an undivided heart. Far too many Christian leaders who have been praised and revered have had profound failings exposed after decades of hidden wrongdoing and deceit. Wherever our lives fail in any of these respects we need to bring them to God and ask for forgiveness and help. If wrongs fester, especially unacknowledged, they can harm the Church every bit as much now as they did in the time of Jesus. They can also smear the truth of the Gospel for those who long to hear it.

Today we face an increasing post-truth ethos, which says there is no truth independent of us. A cynical culture believes something only when someone in authority has denied it. This means that lies become woven into national life not as aberrant but as normal. We have lived through a period where lies have trickled off the tongues of leading politicians in many parts of the world as easily as a leaking tap drips water, yet millions remain indifferent. The message here is to political leaders, for they all hold their offices by permission of God. We have seen so many examples in the last two decades of influential leaders abandoning truth, directing people astray and even putting lives in danger. Jesus so aptly teaches us that whatever their motivation our response must be to reject them and act only on what is right.

Standing up against bad rulers and their regimes has produced martyrs throughout the ages. Sometimes, the simplest and gentlest actions bring wicked reprisals. During the horrendous attack on Ukraine by President Putin's Russian forces, Ukrainian Christians faced difficult choices. A

forty-five-year-old Orthodox village priest, Rostyslav Du-
darenko, had already refused to capitulate to bullies and
held services in the open air when the Ukrainian Orthodox
Church was 'disallowed' by the Russians and their buildings were annexed. During the heavy fire on Ukraine in
March 2022 he was in the woods, near a checkpoint, offering spiritual help to a local volunteer civilian resistance
group. As the Russian tanks approached, he came out of the
woods, raised a cross above his head and quietly went forward to speak to the soldiers. He was unarmed. We shall
never know what truth he wanted to share with them, because they simply shot him dead.

A more widespread problem for our churches today is
that we compartmentalize. We often fail to see that the
kingdom of God applies to the whole of our lives and we
are unaware that a secular, materialist mindset has gripped
so much of our thinking. It's a mistake to think that even
faithful believers in our time are not profoundly shaped by
the narratives of postmodernity, for sadly we are. Much of
the culture we live in sees the universe as without transcen-
dental meaning or eternal purpose. The belief that there
is no overarching metanarrative to which we must submit
can find a hearing in the Church also. Consequently, we are
all invited to define our own concept of existence. The effect of culture on the Church is that often doubt is elevated above faith, and disciplined Christian living is ridiculed.
It is not even unheard of for some Christians to deny the
reality of sin and see it as an obsession of an old era. But
this means also denying the reality of God's redemption
in Christ. However much it goes against the grain of our

culture, God asks us to live lives of integrity and truth. And we are not excused if our faith is so hollow that we do not believe in judgement. So much of Matthew's Gospel tells us the opposite. As we read in chapter 10, whatever we have said in the dark will be heard in the light, and what we have whispered behind closed doors will be shouted from the rooftops. Cover-up is not possible in the kingdom of heaven.

Warnings and the 'last days' (24.1 – 25.46)

Jesus' woes to religious leaders and his lament over Jerusalem turn into dire warnings and predictions of calamities. We can be puzzled about the timescale. Some refer to the destruction of the Temple, which will happen within the lifetime of some of Jesus' hearers, and some refer to the end of the age, when Christ will return. In several places Matthew seems to acknowledge that these will not take place in the same temporal period, so why does he often put them together?

Dick France suggests that it is because there is a close theological connection between the two: 'Both are aspects of the consummation of Jesus' ministry, both involve a judgement which will vindicate him as God's true and last word to his people.'[2] Matthew doesn't intend us to telescope nearer and distant events into one massive series of happenings, but where there are specific time references in Jesus' warnings, he sees them as applying to the coming judgement on Jerusalem.

Matthew's text hints at the great contrast between what Jerusalem was then and what it would be. The disciples were the first to hear of it. They were clearly overawed by the magnificence of the Temple of Jerusalem. As Galilean fishermen, they knew the lake and country region far better than the city, and urban architecture would have seemed impressive. In particular, the Temple building must have been incredibly spectacular. Located 60 metres (200 ft) above the Kidron Valley and said to have taken up one sixth of the city, it dominated the skyline and terrain. So Jesus' prophecy that it would be brought completely to ruin must have startled them enormously. How could such magnificence be brought to rubble? Yet there was more; its annihilation was to foreshadow many other kinds of destruction. The devastating scenario of nations at war, earthquakes, catastrophes and famines must have sounded terrifying.

Jesus looks back to an apocalyptic passage in Daniel that speaks of the 'abomination that causes desolation' (9.26–27). Many believe this refers to sacrilegious acts of the idolatrous Seleucid king Antiochus IV in the second century BC. It was a time never to be forgotten. Josephus describes the impact of the king's idolatry on the Temple after he got possession of the city:

[H]e left the temple bare and took away the golden candle sticks and the golden altar and table . . . when the king had built an idol altar upon God's altar he slew swine upon it and so offered a sacrifice neither according to the law nor the Jewish religious worship in that country. He also compelled them to forsake the worship which they paid to their own gods and adore those who he took to be gods and made them build temples and raise idol alters in every city and village . . .[3]

Jesus foresees a repetition of what Daniel described in a new desecration of the Temple, when another enemy ruler would devastate Jewish people. Terror and affliction, the urgent rush out of homes, fleeing to the mountains, the particular vulnerability of pregnant and nursing women all speak of mass panic in the face of horrendous suffering and carnage.

His prophecy fits well the First Jewish Revolt against the Romans of AD 66–70. It erupted after decades of hostility when Florus, the last Roman procurator, stole huge quantities of silver and gold from the Temple. The outraged resistant Jews rioted, and the Zealots made some early gains against the Romans, but their towns and villages were ravaged, people slaughtered and the eventual outcome was inevitable. The siege of Jerusalem in AD 70 was probably one of the worst sieges in history. Josephus describes the final days when whole families were starved to death:

> The partisans were no longer in a position to help; everywhere was slaughter and flight. Most of the victims were peaceful citizens, weak and unarmed, butchered wherever they were caught. Round the Altar the heaps of corpses grew higher and higher, while down the Sanctuary steps poured a river of blood and the bodies of those killed at the top slithered to the bottom.

The blood ran down the streets, putting the fires out. Over a million Jewish people died during this period. That horrific time in Israel's history does indeed fit the prediction given by Jesus.

It seems that many other destructive periods will unfold before the Messiah returns. Jesus lists wars, rumours of wars, earthquakes and famines as all marking the 'beginning of birth-pains' (24.8), but the end is not yet. He makes it clear that no one knows when that will be. Yet he is unambiguous about the things that will happen in the disciples' own lifetime, not least their persecution. The disciples would have grasped by now that suffering was to be on their agenda, but everything Jesus had already told them was now coming closer to realization. They would face hatred, torture and death. The integrity of the Church itself could be threatened. The temptation to betray fellow believers, to follow false leaders and fall away from the faith was all part of the challenges ahead.

I suspect that at the beginning of their time with Jesus the disciples did not expect persecution any more than most readers of this book expect persecution. But it would happen, and become a persistent pattern for followers of Jesus over centuries to come. The scenario described by Jesus is a clear reflection of the plight experienced by millions of believers in the 'suffering Church' today. Across the world, many of Jesus' followers undergo discrimination, persecution, incarceration and death for professing faith in Christ. Organizations like Open Doors work to support them and expose the injustices. The challenge remains for Christians everywhere to stand firm, identify compassionately with those who suffer and work together for God's kingdom. As Christ also foretold, the good news of the kingdom continues to be proclaimed. The Gospel is preached power-fully across the globe today, often through the suffering of faithful believers who endure to the end.

Preliminary to the 'end times' will be the rise of false prophets, cult founders and fake messiahs. Throughout the last century many random cults grew up, with their leaders propagating immorality and even mass suicide. In our own times, millions of people have become caught up in far-fetched conspiracy theories like QAnon, whose adherents have made inroads into even the Church. Jesus warned us not to be taken in by myths and by those who claim sightings of the Messiah. They will always draw us away from the truth.

The return of the 'Son of Man' will be heralded also by 'great tribulation' and cataclysmic events, affecting our whole planet. In our own age, the rise of nationalism, conflict, global disasters, climate change, even pandemics, can point us back to his prophecy. As we note the dramatic events of our world, many believe that the end times may well be drawing close.

Yet even though he urges us to read the signs, Jesus insists that we cannot tell when he will return and the end will come. The hour of that event is known to God alone. It is not for us to speculate on dates or times. Our task is to live with the reality of his coming and be watchful. Jesus warns us that the people who will be most taken unawares will be those who never give a thought to God and whose lives are consumed by worldly existence. He points to the unreadiness of Noah's neighbours before the flood, and tells a parable of the bad servant oblivious to his master's impending return. We should never lapse into complacency.

Jesus' final parables in Matthew all focus on the need to be ready for his return and the consequences of our indifference to what God asks of us.

The parable of the foolish virgins

We understand this parable better when we see it in context and understand that 'virgin' simply means 'young woman' and the ten in the story are invited weddings guests, probably friends of the bride. When a couple married, the whole community was involved and the party could last for days. It was normal for the bridegroom to keep his guests (and bride) waiting, sometimes beyond nightfall. When the bridegroom's arrival was signalled, everyone would rush to meet him, lighting their torches if necessary. Because, in this story, no one knew the wedding time in advance, people needed to stay prepared, but half the bride's friends didn't. They dropped off to sleep. Fair enough, they were tired. But worse, they had no oil for their lamps. They couldn't borrow oil as others needed it, so with no way of going to greet the bridegroom, they missed the glorious festivities of the wedding. Jesus' reference was clear. The whole history of Israel was preparation for the coming of God's Son. But though warmly invited, their unpreparedness could mean their exclusion when he returned.

For us, preparation is as urgent as it was for the young wedding guests. It's too late to start preparing when everything is underway. And as biblical scholar William

Barclay has remarked, some things cannot be borrowed. None of us can borrow a relationship with God; we must have our own. The consequences for the young women were that they missed a great party. The consequences of being unready for Christ's return are very much more serious.

The parable of the talents

A talent was a weight, valuable according to the metal used to make it. We don't know its value in this story, but we do know that the talents were distributed unequally in proportions of five, two and one. Jesus was not reinforcing status or inequality in this story, but simply describing how things are: humans differ. We all have gifts, however, and what matters is not their quality or number, but what we do with them.

The fundamental problem with the useless servant was his attitude. Lacking self-confidence, he could have committed himself to learning more and trying harder, but instead he grumbled, complained and was bitter. He envied those better endowed and resented his master. Yet the master placed no impossible demands on him. He asked only that the servant work within his ability and develop what he had. By putting his talent in a hole, to be returned intact but unchanged, the servant ignored the trust placed in him. The outcome was proof of the idea 'use it or lose it' – loss for him and gain for the one who worked hard.

Sometimes in the Church we prefer things to stay as they are rather than use our gifts to bring the changes God wants. The result is that things change anyway, but we are not part of it. Here, the master isn't rewarding a class of elite, indolent people. God has entrusted all of us with gifts and asks everyone to use them well. We will all have accounting to do and be judged when Christ returns.

The parable of the sheep and the goats

This is a chilling parable at many levels. Those who come before the judgement seat of God are divided not by what they profess or believe, but by the way they put their faith into action. And the judgement is not related to the correctness of their theology or the sermons they've preached, but to their compassion. Those affirmed by God are motivated by love for others, especially the vulnerable. Those rebuked are indifferent. The story thus warns against apathy and complacency, and challenges the illusions we might have about ourselves.

Notice in the story how easy it seems to be to win God's approval. He does not commend people's great achievements. The actions Jesus lists are not costly, except in terms of time and effort. They are things anyone can do. We can all share food and drink, welcome strangers, provide clothing and visit the sick and imprisoned. We only need kindness and humility. Those who reached out were unselfish, not performing to get something back, not wanting applause. Those who did nothing were unconcerned about others, oblivious to their needs or suffering. They would have done these things, they say, if they had realized they would get God's approval. But that's still self-centredness – not compassion.

So the parable is a challenge to us all. God sees our actions, knows our hearts and wants us to serve him. We do that best not just by preaching but also putting faith into action, showing consistent neighbourly love. When we live like this, we live in constant preparation for Christ's return.

In all these parables it is clear that the return of the Messiah does not simply mark the ending of our world. It also brings judgement. This is particularly hard for our generation to hear, because judgement is such an unpopular concept. Many, even in the Church, exclude God's judgement from their thinking and focus only on love. Yet they are bound up together. God's love for the vulnerable is expressed in judgement on the evil that harms them. The unfaithful servant is openly judged by God, not only because of his complacency, but also because of his cruelty and injustice. When we are indifferent to the needs of those who suffer, we compound their pain.

In Jesus' woes and warnings and prophecies of the end of time, Matthew leaves us with three distinct messages. First, we should be people of integrity who serve God and other people, not hypocrites or deceivers, preoccupied with ourselves. Second, we should ignore those who think they have worked out God's plan for the future and can forecast when Christ will return. They cannot. We can read the signs and know the prophecies, but only God knows when it will happen. Third, we should not brush off the urgency. The way Satan undermines people's active faith most effectively is by telling them not that there is no God or there is no hell, but that there is no hurry. Instead, we are to live today in readiness for Christ's return.

6

Meeting God in Christ's suffering, death and resurrection

The German theologian Martin Kähler described Mark's Gospel as a 'passion narrative with an extended introduction'.[1] And indeed, about a third of Mark's Gospel focuses on the last week of Jesus' life, on his betrayal, suffering and death. The proportion is smaller in Matthew's Gospel, because the focus on teaching and fulfilment of prophecy is much bigger. Yet Matthew certainly sees these events as the climax of his narrative. Almost everything Mark records in chapters 14–15 is found in Matthew 26–27.

The Passion chapters begin with Jesus telling his disciples that the time has finally come. His many warnings to them about his impending death have been heading towards this point. Matthew reinforces Jesus' words by taking us backstage to hear the conspiracy between the chief priests and elders. The question is no longer 'if' they will have Jesus arrested, but 'when and where'. The Passover festival is ruled out, because they fear the crowds and the possibility of a riot in protest.

Matthew moves us on to two contrasting incidents: an act of generosity and trust from a woman, and an act of greed and treachery from a disciple. The see-saw now between

Jesus and the authorities, love and betrayal, assurances and failure, depicts the contest between goodness and evil highlighted throughout the rest of the Gospel.

Matthew's account of the woman anointing Jesus parallels those given by Mark and John. Luke's account is different. As in the other Gospels, her action here causes consternation, this time over the alleged extravagant waste. The plea that the money involved could have been given to the poor cuts no ice with Jesus. They have plenty of opportunities to serve the poor, he says, for the poor are always with them. Instead, he calls her action 'beautiful'. For him it's a symbolic, loving preparation of his body for burial. What is more, history will mark her generosity, for wherever the Gospel is preached, she will be remembered.

The contrast between the actions of this woman, unnamed in Matthew, and the significant actions of Judas is substantial at every level. We don't know the woman's relationship with Jesus, only that she cares enough to lavish her precious oils on his body. We do know that Judas is Jesus' disciple, yet he cares so little that he colludes with Jesus' enemies. The woman's anointing prepares Jesus' body for burial. Judas also prepares his body for burial, but through infidelity and betrayal. The woman gives, pouring out love. Judas takes, exchanging Jesus for 30 pieces of silver. Even here, Matthew knows that his readers will see the reference. In Zechariah 11.12, that same sum is 'weighed out' (NRSV) as the wages of the rejected shepherd who was a messianic figure. Wherever the Gospel is preached, history will certainly mark Judas also, but as the one who betrayed Jesus.

Today, people often ask whether Judas can really be held to blame. When Jesus said it would be better for the betrayer that he had never been born (26.24) was that really fair? Since Christ's death was essential for the salvation of the world, surely Judas's betrayal was theologically necessary? But this is a false dilemma. What Judas did was profoundly wrong, and he chose to do it; it was his decision. God brought salvation through Christ's death, but it could have happened in any number of ways. God does not put sin in people's hearts – neither Judas's nor ours. We are responsible for our sin. Of course we cannot explain the connection between what happens inside our time and God's cosmic time; the paradox of God's sovereign purposes and human responsibility is echoed in the disciples' preaching (Acts 2.23; 3.13–19). Yet, however we look at it, Judas himself bore the guilt of treachery and betrayed the one who loved him.

The Last Supper

Matthew tells us nothing about the man who provided the place of hospitality for Jesus and his disciples to celebrate the Passover. He is simply referred to as 'a certain man'. Although he clearly knew Jesus, he may never have known the full significance of their gathering. Most of the disciples didn't either, at least not entirely. Judas had clearly managed to hide what he had been doing from his fellow disciples. So they ate and drank together in apparent peace. But Judas could not hide his intentions from Jesus, and he soon became aware that Jesus knew. The public announcement that one of them would betray him was clearly a party-stopper.

It feels unnerving when each of the disciples asks Jesus if it could be him. Could they all have been capable of betrayal? Though eleven of them had no such intention, they seemed to lack the confidence in their own righteousness to rule it out. Or maybe it was true humility that enabled them to recognize their ability to sin. Judas asked the question too, but hypocritically, for he knew the answer and Jesus confirmed it. Jesus' reference to one who 'dipped his hand in the bowl with me' is an indication of the closeness of their relationship, and the depth of the betrayal that would take place. Yet even Jesus' pronouncement of 'woe' on the one who was to betray him did not stop Judas.

Matthew's narrative again opens our own self-reflection. Many of us are probably only dimly aware of the wrong things we are capable of doing. Much of the time we are able to hide our sins and failings from others, even those who are very close to us. Which of us is a truly open book to our friends and family? Which of us has no thoughts or attitudes we would want sometimes to conceal from others? Some people are very skilled at hiding; they can live with all kinds of deceit and pretence. Some even eventually begin to inhabit the alternative reality they have constructed about themselves. But truth is real. Judas found he could not hide from Jesus and nor can we. God sees our hearts and knows our motivations. When we can live in peace with that knowledge, we realize we are no longer running from God.

Jesus sometimes did things pregnant with symbolic meaning. His entry into Jerusalem had shown him as Servant King, to be received with welcome. This Passover meal is similar. The Passover feast was a celebration of the Jews' deliverance from captivity. The blood of the sacrificial lamb, placed on their doorposts, would ensure their safety as the angel of death passed over. Now, through his words to his disciples, Jesus identifies himself with the Passover lamb. It's his body, his blood, that will bring safety and deliverance. In sealing the new covenant with God, Jesus discloses himself as the Saviour from sin. He gives the bread and the cup to his disciples, inviting them to eat and drink. They would not have known it was the beginning of a sacramental act that would continue through time. Two millennia later, across the globe, we join with them symbolically in Communion. We eat and drink in faith, remembering that Last Supper and the events that followed. With his disciples then and now, we receive Christ's broken body and blood shed for us.

Going out to the Mount of Olives, Jesus had new information for his disciples. They would desert him. In the intensity and apprehension, it must have been very uncomfortable to hear that prediction. But after the celebratory meal and joyful singing, Peter's confidence was strong. He was sure Jesus had got this wrong. His response showed that he had not heard Jesus' allusion to his resurrection and Galilee. He was stuck at the suggestion that he would run away and wanted to correct this immediately. Peter would never desert Jesus! But Jesus knew better, and his prophetic words delivered the precise, detailed scenario of Peter's denial. The memory of that exchange probably stayed with the disciple for ever.

It is comforting to read of Jesus' compassionate attitude towards the disciples, for we know from the Gospels that it is extended to us. He did not reproach them, even though he knew they would desert him. Even when Peter contradicted him, Jesus didn't respond with disapproval or contempt. He simply described the outcome with clear, factual accuracy. Peter thought his love for Christ and his faith in him was strong enough to withstand all eventualities. He was wrong. God knows that our weaknesses will lead us to sin also. Those of us who are believers can easily be self-assured about our own discipleship. Yet, like Peter, we are only safe when we replace confidence in our own strength and ability with the humility of depending on God alone.

The garden of Gethsemane

It is time for Jesus to pray. One unnamed friend had provided Jesus with the upper room, now another gives him access to an olive garden, where he retreats with Peter, James and John. Jesus knows he is going to die a barbaric death and must overcome his fear and trust the Father. But this is not easy. He wrestles in prayer, pleading three times for some other way. We see the agony and intensity of Jesus' praying. Luke's Gospel describes it as being like sweating great drops of blood. He empties himself of any residual self-will before finally conceding, 'My Father . . . your will be done.'

We see the loneliness too of Gethsemane in this passage. The three disciples, the same who were with him to witness the transfiguration, are asked to keep watch with him. They start out alert, but soon fail miserably. When Jesus finds them sleeping he characteristically asks them now not to pray for him, but for themselves. Their lack of commitment to him in his greatest hour of need makes them more vulnerable to attacks from the evil one. The impact on Jesus, however, is to increase his sense of isolation. He has to face the terror of unleashed hatred in the loneliness of his own soul. As Ronald Rolheiser says, 'in the Garden of Gethsemane, Jesus dies before he dies and in that way readies himself for what awaits him'. So his friends sleep on, and Jesus disturbs them only when the time for his betrayal has come.

The disciples arise from their sleep; Jesus arises from his knees. They go on to an ordeal that Jesus has wrestled with but the three others are completely unprepared for. Jesus is ready, having been in deep prayer. This speaks to us of its great importance. In prayer, Jesus has subordinated his own human will to God's higher authority and found the peace that will enable him to face death. Rolheiser continues, helping us to see how crucial this is for us all:

> When Jesus left the Last Supper room he couldn't do it. That was the great transition. Only after he had broken down, had sweated the blood, had told his father many times 'I don't want to do this,' he finally broke down and accepted it. How many of us in our own way experience that frustration, that same sense of abandonment? Yet at the moment of acceptance, God's liberating grace flows.[2]

Jesus reveals so transparently that for us to be able to stand in defiant courage before evil, we too need first to have knelt in fervent prayer before God.

Betrayal

The story of Jesus' betrayal is more complex than it seems. Judas had given crucial information to Jesus' enemies, especially the time and place when he would be away from crowds. Judas offered to identify him with a kiss of greeting. Yet Jesus would have needed little identification. He was well known, so it is strange that this was necessary. And when Judas does kiss Jesus, the word in Greek changes. It's not a kiss of 'greeting' but one that signifies something of 'repeated passionate embrace'. Why? Was Judas struggling emotionally himself with the terror of what he was doing? Some commentators suggest that Judas fervently wanted Jesus to make a show of divine strength, to call down the angels and demonstrate his power. Whatever Judas's ultimate motives were, however, Jesus called him 'betrayer'.

Jesus' arrest symbolizes the warfare of peace and truth against violence and lies. No peace comes with Judas's kiss. Instead he effectively heads up a lynch mob, reputedly sent by the chief priests and elders, but clearly outside the law. It quickly becomes obvious that violence is not Jesus' way and should never be ours. In our own world we find so often that violence brings only further violence. Jesus rebukes the disciple who attacks the servant, and restores the man's ear. In front of armed men he makes it clear he could call angels to blast his enemies. But he doesn't. For us, Christ's way is that of peace, not military might.

Although costly, Jesus made his own response to the arrest. Nothing forced him to go to Jerusalem for Passover. He could have exposed Judas and cut out his betrayal. In the garden he could have quietly slipped away before the mob arrived. Although his life would be taken brutally from him, he laid it down by choice. Foretold by prophets and in the plan agreed between him and the Father, Jesus' death was given for human restoration. God's purposes are worked out only by sacrificial love.

The 'Jewish' trial

Jesus now faces, alone, the mockery of a trial. His disciples have fled; Peter follows and watches from a distance but offers no help or comfort. The trial itself seems to have taken place quickly, presided over by the high priest at his house (26.57). Already assembled was the Sanhedrin, the supreme court of scribes, Pharisees, Sadducees and elders. Sanhedrin regulations, however, decreed that criminal cases should be tried during the daytime, and at its own meeting place in the Temple precinct. No criminal trials should occur during Passover. So this 'trial', if indeed it was one, had seemingly already involved multiple violations of Jewish law. If it was instead a simple ad hoc gathering to enable the Jewish authorities to agree on tactics, it should have had no juridical force.

In a proper trial, two witnesses, examined separately, were required to make compatible allegations. We don't know how many futile attempts were made as the Sanhedrin scoured for evidence. Eventually, two people attested that Jesus claimed he could destroy and rebuild the Temple in three days. This was a distortion of his prophecy about the destruction of the Temple and about his own death and resurrection on the third day. Jesus chose the legal option to remain silent before the lies.

Following the next question, Jesus could have walked away a free man if he had remained silent or denied he was the Messiah. Saying 'yes' invited the charge of blasphemy and a sentence of execution. Yet his answer went even further. He quoted Daniel 7.13 and applied its account of the triumph and glorification of the Messiah to himself. Jesus knew full well what he was doing and Matthew wanted us to witness this climactic declaration. Dick France comments:

> The apparently helpless victim of official suppression is progressively revealed as the builder of the new temple, the Messiah, the Son of God and the one now to be enthroned Lord at God's right hand. A rich irony thus underlies the whole scene and the reader is enabled to see that it is the judges who are judged.[3]

The response was as expected. The high priest's symbolic garment-tearing, the cries of 'blasphemy', the court's violent and ugly scorn, all confirmed the death penalty. Jesus would be bound, led away and sent to Pilate, the Roman governor. The injustice Jesus experienced was mockery thrown in the face of God. An echo of the frenzy and hatred that accompanied the rejection of Christ as God's anointed one has gone down through the centuries and is faced by so many of his faithful witnesses in the persecuted Church today.

Peter and his denial; Judas and his suicide

Jesus' bold confession before the powerful authorities contrasts strikingly with Peter's failure to acknowledge him before the humblest of servants. Peter's denial of Jesus comes so soon after his profession of unflinching loyalty that it's easy to believe his commitment was shallow. His immediate disavowal to the maid, his curses when his Galilean accent identifies him to everyone, and his complete disowning of Jesus form a progressive distancing from the one he swore to honour. Only after his third denial does the cock's crowing remind him of Jesus' prediction. Some suggest this may not have been an actual cockerel crowing, but the name given to the trumpet call that heralded the changing of the Roman guard. But whatever the source, the sound makes Peter painfully aware that Jesus knows him better than he knows himself.

William Barclay sees this passage as an example of the 'staggering honesty of the New Testament' and goes on: 'if ever there was an incident which one might have expected to be hushed up, this was it – and yet here it is told in all its stark shame'.[4] But he also has a more charitable view of Peter, seeing him less as a coward than a man of 'heroic courage'. He didn't flee with the other disciples, but in his desperate desire to stay close to Jesus he put himself at considerable risk. He followed him into danger, into the very courtyard of the high priest's house, and though he denied knowing Jesus to protect himself, his love for Jesus compelled him to stay there. His love was evident in tears of bitter remorse when he realized how badly he had let Jesus down.

Any of us facing perils as followers of Christ might find Peter's emotional and spiritual struggle in our own hearts. So we take comfort from the fact that, despite his cowardice, Peter's faith in Christ never wavered. Barclay believes that the reason this painful story is in the Gospels is because Peter told it to the early Church. He wanted everyone to know that even though he failed Jesus in the hour of greatest need, he was forgiven, restored and entrusted with leadership in the Church. What Jesus did for Peter, he can do for anyone. Peter's story is not of human failure, but of Christ's redemptive and healing love. It applies to us all.

The outcome was quite different for Judas. His was an act of deliberate apostasy rather than a lapse brought about through fear. Now he had to watch as Jesus was passed from the Sanhedrin to the Roman governor, since despite the speed and success of its manipulations the Sanhedrin could not pass the death sentence on Jesus. The Temple elders now had to construct some political charge that Pontius Pilate could not dismiss. In the Temple precinct, Judas watched the destructive plan unfold and realized the outcome that was now inevitable. He brought back the 30 pieces of silver to the chief priests, remorseful over what he had done. But they were in no mood to engage with his regret – he had served their purposes. The money he no longer wanted was contaminating and could only be used to buy a burial ground for unclean bodies. Matthew quotes a prophecy derived from Zechariah 11.13, with more hints of Jeremiah 32.

Flinging blood money into the heart of the Temple was the action of a desperate man now confronted with the gravity of his sin. But though he could hurl the money back, he could not take his own action back. Sin cannot be undone. Its consequences can rarely be avoided. Judas finally recognized the gravity of his betrayal. He had exposed an innocent man to the injustice of those who hated him. Jesus' life would end on a brutal Roman cross. No wonder Judas could no longer live with himself. His suicide marked the realization that his existence was now intolerable.

Judas lived long enough to hate what his sin had bought him. He did what he thought he wanted but came to detest it. This is a common human experience. Sin creates a longing that when fulfilled can so easily become a loathing. But sin can captivate us also and take us into bondage. Thankfully, God invites us to reach out and seek forgiveness for our wrongs. Jesus prayed from the cross even for those who killed him. And those who accept the invitation can, unlike Judas, rejoice that God's grace is greater than human sin.

The Roman trial

Most people in the dock before a judge would have their case well worked out, ready to answer the charges levied against them. An innocent person, especially, would have prepared a cast-iron rebuttal. Yet, other than acknowledging the charge, Jesus again says nothing. Even Pilate is surprised, urging him, without success, to make some response. Pilate, however, was unlikely to have been familiar with Isaiah 53.7 or its significance in his court: 'he did not open his mouth; he was led like a lamb to the slaughter, as a sheep before its shearers is silent, so he did not open his mouth'.

Yet Pilate was impressed by Jesus; his calmness and authority conveyed integrity. Having seen many revolutionaries, Pilate knew that Jesus was not one. He also knew he was

being used by the Jewish religious elite to get rid of someone who made them uncomfortable. The festival custom
of prisoner-release provided the clear answer, reinforced
no doubt by the message from his wife, urging him, 'Don't
have anything to do with that innocent man.' The crowd
would make the obvious choice between this Jesus Messiah
and the violent, brutal criminal Jesus Barabbas. When the
crowd refused Jesus' release, despite being unable to name
any crime he'd committed, Pilate simply gave in. In allowing them to pronounce sentence of death, he plainly abdi-
cated all responsibility.

Washing his hands of the matter did not absolve Pilate
from the injustice of his actions. It can never do that. None
of us can walk away from the responsibilities that are ours,
for God will hold us accountable even if systems don't. Injustice today thrives through dereliction of duty by those
who should judge impartially. Pilate retained responsibility for Jesus' crucifixion, even though he handed it to the
crowd. We too remain answerable, as neighbours or citizens, for the levels of unfairness we ignore or encourage.

The trial of Jesus looked like a victory for injustice, but
Rolheiser feels it was something else:

> Jesus is on trial, but the story is written in such a way
> that, in effect, everyone is on trial, except Jesus. The
> Jewish authorities who orchestrated his arrest are on
> trial for their jealousy and dishonesty. The Roman
> authorities who wield the final power on the matter
> are on trial for their religious blindness. Jesus' friends
> and contemporaries are on trial for their weakness and

betrayal. Those who challenge Jesus to invoke divine power and come off the cross are on trial for their superficial faith. And, not least, each of us is on trial for our own weaknesses, jealousies, religious blindness, and superficial faith. The transcript of the trial of Jesus reads like a record of our own betrayals.[5]

Human failings have not changed much in 2,000 years. The trial is a challenge to us to see what we, both corporately and personally, might be indicted for.

The crucifixion and death of Jesus

There is nothing humane in crucifixion. The flogging of Jesus would have left him bleeding, lashed and barely able to function. The soldiers epitomized the worst of human nature in their awful degrading humiliation and scorn. Nothing resembling respect or compassion was offered to Jesus – just mockery, gratuitous violence, ugliness and hatred. Even forcing Simon of Cyrene (a city in North Africa) to carry his cross was no concession. Jesus was so weak he could not have otherwise made it to execution. Yet carrying Christ's cross may have been a life-changing experience for Simon's family. Mark names his sons, Alexander and Rufus, in his Gospel, suggesting that they were known as Christian followers at the time Mark was writing.

We are horribly familiar with the details of the crucifixion – the impaling of Jesus' body on the cross, the nails driven through his hands, his refusal of the drugged wine to deaden the pain, the stripping him of his clothes and the soldiers casting lots. We don't know whether his clothes represented financial gain or mere trophies, but Jesus' nakedness does symbolize his utter vulnerability and humiliation as he died. His death was unique, yet he hung in solidarity with all torture victims whose bodies go into spasms and whose bowels release their contents without restraint. Crucified alongside two criminals, the caption signifying him as 'King of the Jews' spoke only of utter irony to the passers-by.

Even now the religious leaders could not leave him to die quietly. Success having gone to their heads, they joined the mocking crowd and convicts. Unbelief is rampant in any age, ours included. People in our society are just as ready to ridicule faith in Christ. His powerlessness on the cross signifies defeat; cynicism proclaims the emptiness of Christian hope as people still echo the sneering of that Good Friday crowd. Yet unbelief always misses the point. It was Christ's persistence in staying on the cross that saw his mission through. It's his victory as the Son of God that has drawn millions to him throughout the ages. It's his death that brings life to us today.

Jesus hung on the cross for five hours, the darkness of the last three culminating in Jesus' cry of abandonment by God: *'Eli, Eli, lema sabachthani?'* It's verse 1 of Psalm 22, penned by King David centuries earlier, predicting many of the elements of the last few hours of Christ's life. Not understanding, well-wishers in the crowd offered him vinegar, and waited, thinking he was calling on a prophet. After his final shout (in John's Gospel: 'It is finished') he died, and an earthquake brought cataclysmic damage to the Temple and tombs, terrifying the guards. Suddenly, they were convinced that Jesus was the Son of God.

What did Jesus really mean by quoting Psalm 22? It seems such a cry of God-forsakenness. Theologians have pondered over those words. Jürgen Moltmann, who has written a great deal on it, feels it is hard for Christians to accept it as a shout of abandonment: 'We shall never be able to get used to the fact that at the centre of the Christian faith there is this cry of the God-forsaken Christ for God. We shall always try to soften down its realities, replacing them by more pious last words.'[6]

Some suggest Christ is identifying fully with human hopelessness and suffering; others, that we are drawn into God's pain. Bonhoeffer, the night before he was executed, wrote:

Christ helps us, not by virtue of his omnipotence, but by virtue of his weakness and suffering . . . The Bible directs people towards the powerlessness and suffering of God. Only the suffering God can help. That is a reversal of what the religious man expects from God. Man is summoned to share in God's sufferings at the hands of a godless world.[7]

Yet Jesus was surely also giving a cry of cosmic spiritual truth. If Jesus was indeed sacrificing himself and being made sin for us (2 Corinthians 5.21), he was experiencing the outcome of that sin in separation from the Father: 'God [in his Son] takes the judgment on the sin of man upon himself. He assigns to himself the fate that men by rights should endure.'[8] But for Moltmann, who acknowledges this, it is not a process at arm's length. The forsakenness is experienced by both Father and Son, the suffering being absorbed into God's own being. 'God does not merely enter into the finitude of men and women; he enters into the situation of their sin and God-forsakenness as well . . . he also accepts and adopts it himself, making it part of his own eternal life.'[9]

The truth is that the God-forsakenness Jesus expressed on the cross was at a level we shall never know. No human being has the capacity to understand how the dynamic relationship between Father, Son and Holy Spirit was affected by the sins of humankind in the crucifixion of Jesus. We do know that Jesus suffered and died to bring grace and God's love to us who don't deserve it. And Matthew's description of the signs that accompanied the death of Jesus reinforces that. The shaking earth, the veil torn in the Temple, with the Holy of Holies opened up to ordinary human access, reveal, symbolically, a new vision of our relationship with God. The effect on death itself was noted. Tombs were broken open, and after the resurrection some who had died were seen alive (27.52–53). It's hardly surprising that the centurion standing in terror, watching the impact, expressed conviction that Jesus was truly God's Son.

It is fitting that the chapter ends with the story of dedicated women. A male disciple had betrayed Jesus, another denied him, and most had fled, yet the women remained to the end. Matthew tells us too that there were many of them, though he names only Mary Magdalene, James and

Joseph's mother Mary, and the mother of the sons of Zebe-dee. The women's devotion speaks to us of the reality of faithfulness despite perplexity, doubt and distress. Their confusion must have been greater than most of us have ever known, yet their persistence gives courage, especially to people struggling with hopelessness and fear. They are showing believers in desperate situations that unwavering commitment is still possible. It is conceivable that any one of us can stay close to Jesus in the worst circumstances of our lives and not lose hope.

It probably suited both the Romans and the Jewish leaders to hand Jesus' body over to Joseph of Arimathea. The Romans avoided having to leave a decaying corpse to be eaten by animals, and the Jewish Passover was not over-shadowed by a hanging crucifixion victim. Being rich, Joseph probably had some status but, more importantly, he had a tomb. Not far from the place of execution, it seems to have been newly hewn out of the rock. Tombs were expensive, so it was generous of Joseph to provide his for Jesus. He did not know, of course, that he would soon get his tomb back!

Matthew details that the tomb was very thoroughly closed up. Joseph himself rolled the massive stone into the deep groove in front of the opening. Once sunk in, the stone could not be rolled back by one person alone. Then, at the request of the chief priests, Pilate made it doubly secure. In sealing it with rope and wax at either side of the entrance, the soldiers ensured no one could tamper with it. Posting a guard outside was the final security; the body imprisoned

135

inside could not be removed. No one would spread false rumours of resurrection.

The resurrection

Every age has had its theories about the body and the tomb. It's not uncommon today to hear people suggest that Jesus wasn't really dead and was later rescued. Yet no one there, watching the crucifixion, had any doubt that Jesus was dead. He had been flogged, tortured, impaled, hung for hours and speared. No one worried that he might be revived! What his enemies feared was either disciples snatching his corpse, or that a miracle might really happen. The wonderful thing for us is that they took such meticulously detailed measures to keep the body in, ruling out all normal possibilities of exit. We are left with knowing that God's miraculous power is the best explanation for what happened next.

Manipulation and injustice dominated everything the religious authorities did to Jesus. William Barclay says they used treachery to lay hold of him, illegality to try him, slander to charge him to Pilate and bribery to silence the truth about him. But despite all their efforts, they failed. For the women who did not yet know that, however, the Sabbath must have felt like an endless wait. They knew they must anoint his precious body and face the grief of confronting the torture imprinted on Jesus. But the question of how to get into the tomb was formidable. When they finally arrived with prepared spices, they were utterly bewildered by what faced them. Shocked, numbed soldiers in disarray and an angel seated on the rolled-back stone conveyed a new, unexpected reality: no body to anoint. As they entered the tomb and saw for themselves that it was empty, the angel's words sank in. They were to tell the disciples that Jesus had risen and would meet them in Galilee.

As the women left to tell the disciples, things happened quickly. When Jesus, very much alive, suddenly appeared to them himself, their old role seemed to be turned on its head. Instead of being those who fulfilled the women's personal, domestic tasks of embalming a corpse, they immediately became the first witnesses to Christ's resurrection. Yet it was surely fitting. The faithful women who had been at the cross and tomb now saw and worshipped the risen Christ. They were appointed personally by him as the first evangelists to proclaim the good news of the most world-changing event in history: that he was indeed risen from the dead.

Jesus empowered the women to be the people he was calling them to be. As his newly appointed ambassadors, they could let go of fear, rejoice in his victory and proclaim the Gospel. The false story about the theft of Christ's body folded as the Holy Spirit communicated the power of Christ's resurrection. When Jesus gave his commission to followers gathered in Galilee, he told them to make disciples of all nations and teach them the way of Christ. It must have seemed an incredibly tall order to a small group of Jewish men and women who had spent their entire lives within a small corner of the earth. Christ spoke to both those who believed and those who doubted; his commission was not based on the strength of faith of his followers, but on his own power. Without Christ's power the disciples could accomplish nothing. With it they could open people's hearts to meet God. And their witness changed the history of the world.

We can be profoundly grateful to God for Matthew's Gospel. He reached out with the good news of the Messiah and the kingdom of heaven to his Jewish Christian community but also far beyond it. God used him to tell the story of Jesus: his incarnation, ministry, atoning death and resurrection. We hear Jesus' teaching, receive his love and celebrate his victory over evil. Matthew reminds believers everywhere that we do not rely on our might, for human weakness is made perfect in Christ's strength, even when wickedness seems to flourish and truth brings persecution. We are not disqualified by our doubts, because God's truth triumphs over the lies of Satan and those in bondage to evil. All power in heaven and on earth is given through Christ, so we need to hold on to the promises he made his disciples, because those promises are also for us today.

Over the last two millennia, billions of people have believed what Matthew has shared in his Gospel. People from societies utterly different from those to whom he originally wrote have read his narrative and been convinced of its truth through the leading of the Holy Spirit. They have found forgiveness and new life through Christ's redemptive love; they have turned from self-preoccupation to kingdom service with Christ. They have grasped that God's calling is not limited to background, age, time or culture, because Jesus, the Christ, empowers all those who believe and trust in him.

In the twenty-first century we know this ourselves. To-day, God continues to commission people afresh, anointing believers throughout the globe to continue the work of the kingdom of heaven in their own era. Today we share the calling of those first eyewitnesses in proclaiming and living out the good news of Christ's sacrificial love and resurrection power. And Christ promises that he will indeed be with us always, even to the end of the world.

Questions for reflection or group discussion

1 Meeting God in fulfilment of prophecy

1 What aspects of Matthew's Gospel would you point
to if you were going to support the claim that it is the
'Jewish' Gospel?

2 What do you see as particularly significant about
the four women (Tamar, Rahab, Ruth and Uriah) in
Matthew's genealogy of Jesus? Who would you include
in your genealogy?

3 Some scholars have dated Matthew's Gospel before the
fall of Jerusalem (that is, before AD 70), while others
have dated it later, around AD 80 to 85. What points
would you raise in favour of each of these dates?

4 How would you describe in your own words the
different ways Matthew uses Old Testament prophecies
to show that Jesus fulfils them? Which of the prophecies
resonate with you most?

5 What strikes you most about the difference between
Matthew's account of the Nativity and the longer
account in Luke's Gospel?

2 Meeting God in preparaton for ministry

1 Why do you think Jesus said he needed to be baptized by
John?

2 How would you describe the main difference between John's baptism and the baptism of the 'Holy Spirit and fire' that he said Jesus would bring?

3 What might be the equivalents for ordinary people today of the three temptations that Jesus faced from the devil?

4 *(For personal reflection only)* What in your life are the temptations you find most difficult to resist? How do you resist them? What might you identify as your 'idols'?

5 Jesus seemed very deliberate in the way he chose his disciples. What do you feel is significant about his choice?

3 Meeting God in the teaching of the kingdom

1 Which of the Beatitudes do you find most difficult to understand and why?

2 How can Christians be salt and light in our world today?

3 Can you describe in your own words what Jesus meant when he talked about the kingdom of heaven? Which of the kingdom parables strike you the most?

4 What did Jesus teach about children? Sketch out your own theology of childhood and compare it to the way we understand childhood in our culture today.

5 Miracles were a normal part of Jesus' ministry and were manifestations of the kingdom. What part do you think miracles play today in the Christian faith and life?

4 Meeting God on the road to Jerusalem

1 Why do you think the ablution laws mattered so much to the scribes and Pharisees? What might be similar things we bother about in our churches today?

2 Why do you think Jesus taught in parables, taking especially the parable about the unforgiving servant and parable about the workers in the vineyard?

3 In your own words, tell the story about the conversation the rich young man had with Jesus and bring out some of the assumptions he had about eternal life.

4 Why do you think Jesus told his disciples so many times about the problems they would face in Jerusalem? What do you think the disciples might have made of this?

5 Matthew tells us about Jesus' entry into Jerusalem to show that he was seen as the promised Messiah. What else does Matthew tell us about the nature of crowds?

5 Meeting God in woes and warnings

1 Retell the incident where Jesus turned the money tables over in the Temple precinct from the point of view of (a) the traders, (b) the Temple authorities, (c) the foreigners coming to worship and (d) his disciples. (This could be done as a group with parts allocated!)

2 Why do you think Jesus' opponents chose the method of asking questions to put him in the wrong, rather than simply making allegations against him?

3 How would you summarize the 'woes' of Jesus to the religious leaders? Why did he regard them as so serious?

4 Some of the prophetic warnings of Jesus were fulfilled in AD 70. Which others do you think might have been

fulfilled since, and which of his prophetic warnings might be relevant today?

5 What strikes you reading the three parables about being ready and preparing to meet God in chapter 25?

6 Meeting God in Christ's suffering, death and resurrection

1 Do you think Jesus' teaching on the heart helps to explain the difference between the woman who anointed him and Judas? What would you pick out as important?

2 Look at the contrasts between Jesus' time in the garden of Gethsemane and the time of his arrest. How would you describe the differences?

3 What does Matthew suggest contributed to the rush to get Jesus executed? Which of these were pressures from the Jewish leaders and which were from the Romans?

4 What is your understanding of Jesus' cry from the cross: 'My God, my God, why have you forsaken me?'

5 The four Gospels give different accounts of women finding the tomb empty and being given the message of resurrection. In what ways are these differences enriching rather than confusing?

Appendix 1

The structure of Matthew's Gospel

Matthew's Gospel is regarded as a carefully structured document that aims to communicate as clearly as possible Jesus' identity, mission, purpose and teachings. To do this, it can be seen to contain three key subdivisions and five main discourses. These are signalled to us by phrases or formulae that Matthew employs to introduce or round off the subdivisions or discourses. So, for example, in 4.17 and 16.21 Matthew writes: 'From that time on Jesus began to . . .' and this repeated phrase breaks up his account into the three subsections.

The three subdivisions can be described as:

- Early events: genealogy, Nativity and other events prior to Jesus' public ministry (1.1 – 4.16);
- Public ministry: Jesus' teaching, parables and miracles; disciples and opponents (4.17 – 6.20);
- The suffering, death and resurrection of Jesus.

A more detailed analysis of the structure focuses on the five major discourses of Jesus' teaching in the Gospel. Some see the fact that Matthew pinpoints five discourses as evidence of his Jewish training, in that this might be an allusion to the Pentateuch – the first five books of the Hebrew Scriptures. The sections themselves interrelate in ways that hark

144

back to the way some of the psalms are structured, where the beginning and the end of the psalm parallel each other but also signify changes of mood or spirit. The first and fifth discourses both take place on a mountain, but the teachings within them contrast quite sharply. The first discourse, the Sermon on the Mount, opens with eight blessings, whereas the fifth discourse (often called the Olivet) opens with eight woes. It is also interesting that the eighth beatitude blesses those who have been persecuted for righteousness, and theirs will be the kingdom of heaven, whereas the eighth woe warns those who do the persecuting that theirs will be the destruction of Jerusalem.

After each of the teaching sections Matthew signs off with 'when Jesus finished saying these things . . .' (7.28; 11.1; 13.53; 19.1; 26.1). A narrative follows where we learn more of the ongoing events in Christ's life and ministry.

Basic scheme of teaching discourses

1 Sermon on the Mount (5 – 7)
2 Instruction to the twelve apostles (10)
3 Parables of the kingdom (13.1–53)
4 Teachings on the Church (18)
5 Teachings on the end times on Mount Olivet (24)

A fuller scheme: discourse and narratives, along with prologue and epilogue

This shows the narratives and stories about Jesus that support and develop the discourses and highlight Jesus' identity.

Prologue

Infancy narrative (1 – 2)

Section 1 (3 – 7)

Narrative (3 – 4)
Discourse: Sermon on the Mount (5 – 7) includes the Beatitudes

Section 2 (8.1 – 11.1)

Narrative (8.1 – 9.34)
Discourse: mission (9.35 – 11.1)

Section 3 (11.2 – 13.52)

Narrative (11.2 – 12.50)
Discourse: parables of the kingdom (13.1–53)

Section 4 (13.54 – 18.35)

Narrative (13.54 – 17.27)
Discourse: church life and order (18)

Section 5 (19 – 25)

Narrative (19 – 22)
Discourse: eschatology (23 – 25), includes the 'woes'

Epilogue

Passion narrative (26 – 28)

Appendix 2

The literary relationships between the first three ('Synoptic') Gospels, showing the material they have in common

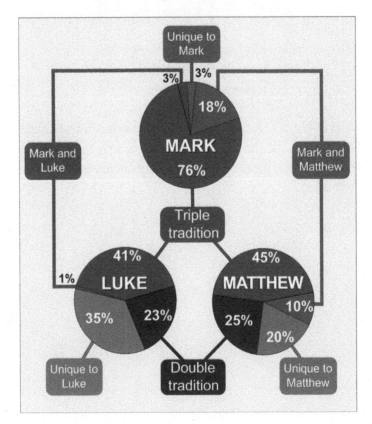

The Gospels' authors have different styles, and their choices of what to include in their accounts are not identical. We would expect this when the Gospels were written down in different periods and by different people. What is remarkable, however, is how much overlap there is in the content:

- 45 per cent of Matthew's material is shared with Mark and Luke;
- 10 per cent of it is found only in Mark;
- 25 per cent is shared only with Luke;
- 20 per cent of it is unique to Matthew.

Most of Mark's Gospel is reflected in Matthew's and Luke's, while Luke's has the largest amount of unique material. The triple tradition gives weight to the argument for the primacy of Mark.

Appendix 3

Source hypotheses

How we explain the similarities and overlaps between the Synoptic Gospels (Matthew, Mark and Luke) has often been referred to as the 'Synoptic problem'. Most scholars reject the idea that the Gospels' accounts of Jesus' life, ministry and death are simply independent of one another, but recognize that there are both significant similarities and interesting differences between them. Consequently, over a very long period, biblical scholars have been offering a number of hypotheses with regard to a common source.

Support for the idea of common sources can be found in the Gospel of Luke. He acknowledges in his prologue to Theophilus that other accounts already exist, and implies that he has used them.

> Many have undertaken to draw up an account of the things that have been fulfilled among us, just as they were handed down to us by those who from the first were eyewitnesses and servants of the word. With this in mind, since I myself have carefully investigated everything from the beginning, I too decided to write an orderly account for you, most excellent Theophilus, so that you may know the certainty of the things you have been taught.
> (Luke 1.1–4)

This suggests that not only was Luke aware that written (and oral) sources based on eyewitness accounts already existed but he had also drawn on them in compiling his own 'orderly account'.

One of the most accepted suggestions, which goes back to the middle of the nineteenth century, is the 'two-source hypothesis' – the idea that the Gospel according to Mark was the main source for Matthew and Luke, but a second source of Jesus' sayings (simply named Q) accounted for material found in Luke and Matthew but not Mark. This hypothesis has been variously developed and expanded. For example, in 1925, B. H. Streeter posited two further sources for material that exists only in Matthew (M) and in Luke (L). (Sometimes this has been referred to as the 'four-source hypothesis'.) Older theories still hold sway with some scholars, especially the Augustinian hypothesis (Matthew's Gospel came first and was the source for Mark; Luke uses both Matthew and Mark) and the Griesbach hypothesis, dating back to the 1780s. The latter is sometimes called the 'two-document hypothesis', and was developed in 1964 by William Farmer. It has probably been the most persistent rival of the two-source hypothesis. It maintains that Matthew's Gospel came first, and both Matthew and Luke were sources for the Gospel of Mark.

For some scholars, one of the problems of the two-source hypothesis has been the positing of Q as the second source. Q is the name given to an assumed collection of material, 'sayings', that accounted for things we find in both Matthew and Luke but not in Mark. Not everyone is comfortable with the idea of a Q source. Austin Farrer wrote 'On Dispensing with Q' in 1955, arguing that there is no need for academics to create a hypothetical source of sayings for what they cannot otherwise explain. He argues, simply, that the Gospel of Mark was written first, followed by the Gospel of Matthew, with Matthew using it as a source material, and then Luke, who used both other Gospels as his source. Later scholars, including Michael Goulder and Mark Goodacre, have picked up Farrer's theory and developed it.

Other scholars have also opted for the primacy of Mark without feeling the need to posit a source for Jesus' sayings. Ralph Wilson sums up the mood when he expresses his impatience with the preoccupation: 'My interest is in the words of Jesus that have come down to us in the New Testament canon, not trying to reconstruct some Q document that is not, and may never have been, in existence.'[1]

Further reading on the 'Synoptic problem'

Collins, Raymond F., *Introduction to the New Testament* (New York: Image Books, Doubleday, 1983).

Dungan, David Laird, *A History of the Synoptic Problem: The canon, the text, the composition, and the interpretation of the gospels* (New Haven, CT: Yale University Press, 1999).

Farmer, William R., *The Synoptic Problem. A critical analysis* (Dillsboro, NC: Western North Carolina Press, 1976).

Goodacre, Mark S., *The Synoptic Problem: A way through the maze,* The Biblical Seminar 80 (Sheffield: Sheffield Academic Press, 2001).

Head, Peter, *Christology and the Synoptic Problem: An argument for Markan priority* (Cambridge: Cambridge University Press, 1997).

Kloppenborg, John S., 'What is Q?' in Q, *The Earliest Gospel: An introduction to the original stories and sayings of Jesus* (Louisville, KY: Westminster John Knox Press, 2008).

Kümmel, Werner Georg, *Introduction to the New Testament*, revised edn, tr. Howard C. Kee (Nashville, TN: Abingdon Press, 1975).

Notes

Introduction

1 See Jeffrey Siker, 'Anti-Semitism and the New
Testament', Oxford Bibliographies, available at: <www.
oxfordbibliographies.com/view/document/obo-
9780195393361/obo-9780195393361-0153.xml>.

2 Michael J. Cook, 'Interpreting "Pro-Jewish" Passages
in Matthew', *Hebrew Union College Annual,* vol. 54
(Cincinnati, OH: Hebrew Union College Press, 1983),
pp. 135–46, available at: <www.jstor.org/stable/23507664>.
Rabbi Cook died in 2021.

3 R. T. France, *Tyndale New Testament Commentaries:
Matthew* (Leicester: IVP, 1985), p. 19.

4 Mark L. Strauss, 'Matthew: Jesus is the Promised Messiah',
Bible Project, available at: <https://bibleproject.com/blog/
gospel-of-matthew>.

5 Graham Stanton, 'The Gospel of Matthew and Judaism',
The Manson Memorial Lecture, delivered in the University
of Manchester on 3 November 1983; published as
edocument, p. 273.

6 Stanton, p. 274.

7 'St Matthew's Gospel', unpublished paper by Professor
Ronald Clements, 2022.

8 Saint Papias, 'Fragments of Papias', in Alexander Roberts,
James Donaldson and A. Cleveland Coxe (eds), *The*

Ante-Nicene Fathers: Volume 1: The Apostolic Fathers with Justin Martyr and Irenaeus (New York: Christian Literature Publishing Company, 1885), p. 155.

9 See Peter Head, *Christology and the Synoptic Problem: An argument for Markan priority* (Cambridge: Cambridge University Press, 1997); Mark S. Goodacre, *The Synoptic Problem: A way through the maze,* The Biblical Seminar 80 (Sheffield: Sheffield Academic Press, 2000); John S. Kloppenborg, 'What is Q?', in *Q, The Earliest Gospel: An introduction to the original stories and sayings of Jesus* (Louisville, KY: Westminster John Knox Press, 2008).

10 John Wenham, *Redating Matthew, Mark and Luke: A fresh assault on the Synoptic problem* (Downers Grove, IL: InterVarsity Press, 1992), p. xxi.

11 France, p. 84.

12 Richard Bauckham, *Jesus and the Eyewitnesses: The gospel as eyewitness testimony* (Grand Rapids, MI: Eerdmans, 2006), pp. 111–12.

13 Steve Hays, 'Triablogue', April 2016, available at: <http://triablogue.blogspot.com/2016/04/the-evidence-for-matthews-authorship.html>.

1 Meeting God in fulfilment prophecy

1 Strauss.

2 Raymond E. Brown, *A Coming Christ in Advent: Essays on the Gospel Narratives: Preparing for the birth of Jesus, Matthew 1 and Luke 1* (Collegeville, MN: Liturgical Press, 1988), p. 21.

3 Ronald Rolheiser, 'The Checkered Origins of Grace', 7 December 2008, available at: <https://ronrolheiser.com/the-checkered-origins-of-grace/#.YiD045PP10s>.

4 Ibid.

5 Ibid.

6 Glenn D. Pemberton, 'Matthew and the Prophets', *Leaven*, vol. 13:2, article 10, 2005, available at: <https://digitalcommons.pepperdine.edu/leaven/vol13/iss2/10>.

7 Strauss.

8 J. Wenham, *Redating Matthew, Mark and Luke: A fresh assault on the synoptic problem* (Downers Grove, IL: InterVarsity Press, 1992), p. 103.

9 John Goldingay, *The Old Testament and Christian Faith: Jesus and the Old Testament in Matthew 1–5*, available at: <https://biblicalstudies.org.uk/article_ot1_goldingay.html>.

10 R. T. France, *Tyndale New Testament Commentaries: Matthew* (Leicester: IVP, 1985), p. 81.

11 See Brown, p. 616. They become more evident when we study them in the light of further revelation and the years that have elapsed.

2 Meeting God in preparation for ministry

1 Josephus, *Antiquities of the Jews*, 18.5.2.

2 Ronald Rolheiser, 'Willpower Alone Is Not Enough', 30 September 2012, available at: <https://ronrolheiser.com/willpower-alone-is-not-enough/#.Ymqt9y1Q3fZ>.

3 Ian Paul, available at: <www.psephizo.com/biblical-studies/the-back-story-to-matthews-account-of-jesus-baptism>.

4 Ibid.

5 Henri Nouwen, *Life of the Beloved: Spiritual living in a secular world* (New York: Crossroad, 1992), pp. 32–6.

6 Ronald Rolheiser, 'Our Three Temptations', 8 July 2007, available at: <https://ronrolheiser.com/our-three-temptations/#.Yh5NfpPP2u4>.

7 C. S. Lewis, *The Four Loves* (London: Geoffrey Bles,1960).

8 William Cowper, 'O! For a Closer Walk with God', 1772.

9 Ronald Rolheiser, 'The Desert – the Place of God's Closeness', 2 April 2000, available at: <https://ronrolheiser.com/the-desert-the-place-of-gods-closeness/#.YmAvOC1Q0_U>.

3 Meeting God in the teaching of the kingdom

1 John Stott, *The Message of the Sermon on the Mount*, The Bible Speaks Today series, revised edn (London: IVP, 2020).

2 Doug Webster, 'The Sermon on the Mount in a Secular Age. Delivered as a video lecture at Beeson Divinity School, Samford University, Birmingham, Alabama, 2 October 2018.

3 Lesslie Newbigin, *The Gospel in a Pluralist Society* (Grand Rapids, MI: Eerdmans, 1989), p. 9.

4 See Ed Walker, *A House Built on Love* (London: SPCK, 2018).

5 R. T. France, *Tyndale New Testament Commentaries: Matthew* (Leicester: IVP, 1985), p. 177.

6 Charles Haddon Spurgeon, 'The Triumphal Entry into Jerusalem', Sermons: Matthew 21:5, from *Metropolitan Tabernacle Pulpit*, vol. 7, 18 August 1861, available

at: <www.spurgeon.org/resource-library/sermons/the-triumphal-entry-into-jerusalem>.

7   A. B. du Toit, 'The Kingdom of God in the Gospel of Matthew', available at: <www.researchgate.net/publication/273357401_The_Kingdom_of_God_in_the_Gospel_of_Matthew>.

8   Herman N. Ridderbos, *The Coming of the Kingdom* (Ontario, Canada: Paideia Press, 1978), pp. 354–5.

4 Meeting God on the journey to Jerusalem

1   R. T. France, *Tyndale New Testament Commentaries: Matthew* (Leicester: IVP, 1985), p. 243.

2   Often called the 'Matthean exception' (to a universal prohibition on divorce).

3   Deuteronomy 24.1–3. See also Isaiah 50.1, Jeremiah 3.8.

4   Rosemary Radford Ruether, *To Change the World* (New York: Crossroad, 1981), p. 50.

5   John Piper, 'He Set His Face to Go to Jerusalem', 4 April 1982, available at: <www.desiringgod.org/messages/he-set-his-face-to-go-to-jerusalem>.

6   Commentators query whether one or two donkeys was intended by Zechariah, pointing out the Hebrew parallelism here. But Matthew would certainly have understood Hebrew parallelism and still opted for the latter.

7   Eddie Askew, *Facing the Storm* (Brentford, Middlesex: Leprosy Mission International, 1989).

8   Charles Haddon Spurgeon, 'The Triumphal Entry into Jerusalem', Sermons: Matthew 21:5 from *Metropolitan Tabernacle Pulpit*, vol. 7, 18 August 1861, available

at: <www.spurgeon.org/resource-library/sermons/
the-triumphal-entry-into-jerusalem/#flipbook>.

5 Meeting God in woes and warnings

1 R. T. France, *Tyndale New Testament Commentaries:
   Matthew* (Leicester: IVP, 1985), p. 330.
2 France, p. 334.
3 Josephus, *Antiquities of the Jews*, XII.5.4.

6 Meeting God in Christ's suffering, death and resurrection

1 Martin Kähler, *The So-called Historical Jesus and the
   Historic Biblical Christ* (Minneapolis, MN: Fortress Press,
   1988), p. 80, n. 11.
2 Ronald Rolheiser, 'Agony in the Garden: Understanding
   the passion of Jesus', Catholic Update, February 2008,
   Franciscan Media.
3 R. T. France, *Tyndale New Testament Commentaries:
   Matthew* (Leicester: IVP, 1985), p. 377.
4 William Barclay, *Barclay's Daily Study Bible*: Matthew 26,
   available at: <www.studylight.org/commentaries/eng/dsb/
   matthew-26.html>.
5 Ronald Rolheiser, 'Our Own Good Friday', 8 April 2019,
   available at: <https://ronrolheiser.com/our-own-good-
   friday/#.Ym7q7i1Q2fU>.
6 Jürgen Moltmann, *Jesus Christ for Today's World*
   (Minneapolis, MN: Fortress Press, 1994), p. 35.
7 Dietrich Bonhoeffer, *Letters and Papers from Prison*
   (Minneapolis, MN: Fortress Press, 2010), p. 479.

8 Jürgen Moltmann, *The Crucified God: The cross of Christ as the foundation and criticism of Christian theology* (Minneapolis, MN: Fortress Press, 1993), p. 195.
9 Jürgen Moltmann, *The Trinity and the Kingdom: The Doctrine of God* (Minneapolis, MN: Fortress Press, 1993).

Appendix 3

1 Ralph F. Wilson, The Jesus Walk Bible Study Series, available at: <Jesuswalk.com>.

TWENTY-FIVE EMPOWERING STORIES FROM THE BIBLE

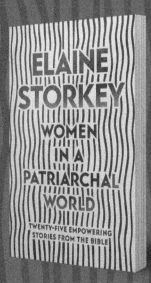

'This is a book full of wisdom. It is warm, encouraging, strong and inspiring – just like its author.'
CHURCH TIMES

'Blows wide open the all-too-common assumption that women in the Bible always bowed to a patriarchal system.'
JULIA BICKNELL, FORMER BBC JOURNALIST FOR *WOMAN'S HOUR*

'These familiar stories erupt like gentle fireworks bringing fresh illumination, excitement, colour and impact.'
OPEN DOORS

'Each page left me feeling more empowered than the last.'
PRESS RED

9780281084074 | PAPERBACK & EBOOK | 144 PAGES

spck publishing